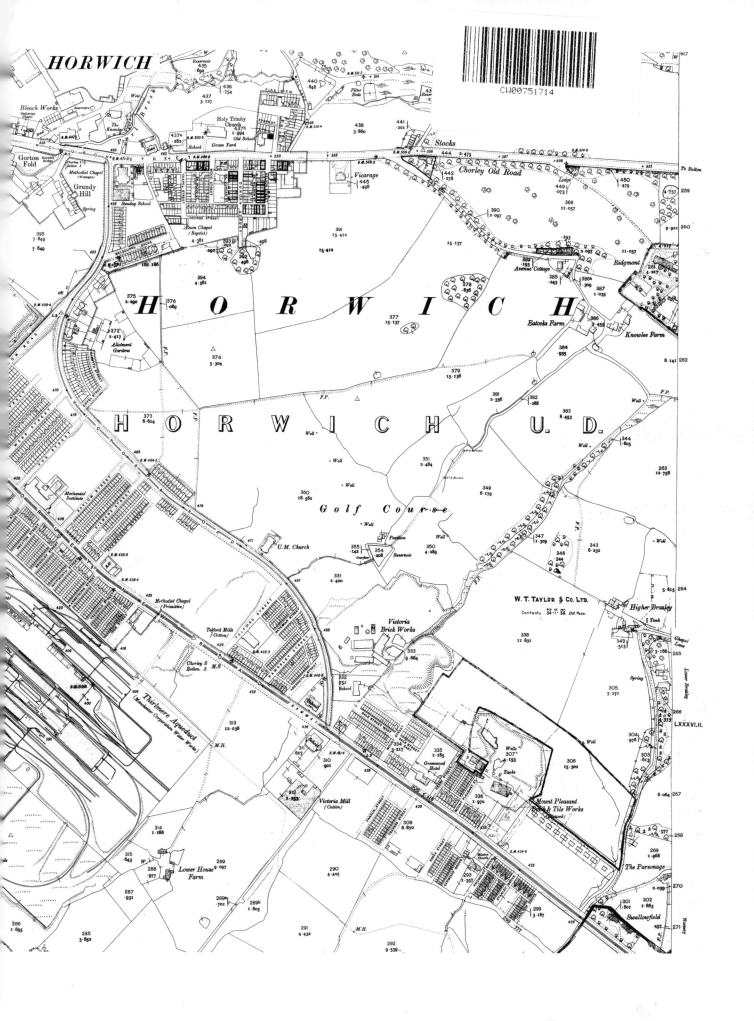

DEDICATION
"REMEMBER ME TO HORWICH"

Mr. H. E. O'Brien.

"Horwich was a great railway town. Its engineers were inventive and efficient. They made a big contribution to the development of the railways. The people were the best. So friendly. So good hearted. I have never forgotten them".

Col. H. E. O'Brien, DSO, Works Manager at Horwich Locomotive Works. 1910-1924

Aerial view of Horwich Locomotive Works. c.1930.

HORWICH LOCOMOTIVE WORKS

by
M. D. Smith
in collaboration with E. M. Brownlow

Horwich Locomotive Works Paint Shop. c.1950.

Wyre Publishing

North Villas, Garstang Road, St. Michael's on Wyre, Lancashire, PR3 OTE
ISBN 0-9526187-2-9

OPPORTUNITY

"I shall pass through this world but once - any good therefore that I can show to any human being, let me do it now. Let me not defer or neglect it, for I shall not pass this way again."

ACKNOWLEDGEMENTS

My first duty is to record appreciation to my wife Andrea for her help and support, and for the assistance of Martin Brownlow who has collaborated with me in the publication of this work.

The undermentioned have also contributed in a variety of ways and without their help the finished result would not have been possible. I am pleased to record sincere thanks for their kindness to:

Jill M. Aldersley . . . . .Ambleside, Cumbria.
Joan Birchall . . . . .Foxholes, Horwich.
Edward Brownlow . . . . .Brownlow Road, Horwich.
George Bush . . . . .Mary Street West, Horwich.
Albert Clayton . . . . .St. Michael's on Wyre.
Arthur Danks . . . . .Chorley New Road, Horwich.
Geoffrey Drinkwater . . . . .Lever Park Avenue, Horwich.
John Garrity . . . . .Burlingham's Park, Garstang.
Darren Hickey . . . . .Mill Hill, Rivington.
James Hickey . . . . .R.M.I. Club, Horwich.
Stephen Leyland . . . . .Walker Avenue, Bolton.
Derek Lunt . . . . .Hurst Building, Horwich Business Park.
Brenda Mitchell . . . . .Stocks Park Drive, Horwich.
Robert Molloy . . . . .Whitton Mews, Horwich.
Norman Pendlebury . . . . .Darley Street, Horwich.
Eric Stutchbury . . . . .Tomlinson Street, Horwich.
John Winnard. . . . . .Chorley New Road, Horwich.
Bolton Evening News
British Rail.

First Published 1996
Copyright © 1996 M. D. Smith.

All rights reserved. No part of this publication may be reproduced, stored in a retrieval system, transmitted in any form, by any means electronic or mechanical, or photocopied, or recorded by any other information storage and retrieval system without prior permission in writing from the author.

Typesetting by Highlight Type Bureau Ltd, Bradford
Printed by The Amadeus Press Ltd, Huddersfield

TABLE OF CONTENTS

(continued)

INTRODUCTION

The story of Horwich Locomotive Works is a fascinating subject which has long been deserving of a dedicated history. A number of excellent railway publications do in fact contain references to the Works but in a wider context amongst other issues.

In the mid 1800's the village of Horwich nestled peacefully at the foot of a Pennine spur. The highway rate was fourpence (2p) in the £1 and these dues were collected by an old farmer whose approach was always signalled well in advance by the sound of his enormous clogs on the cobblestones. He was reputed to have made his footwear comfortable by stuffing them with as much hay as would fodder a calf. On a summer evening it was pleasant to walk through Sharrock's Farm (on which land the locomotive works was eventually built) to the Ridgway Collieries, which provided employment for many of the villagers.

When the Lancashire and Yorkshire Railway Company purchased the site for Horwich Locomotive Works on the 27th May 1884, a chain of events was put in motion which upgraded Horwich to township status and affected the lives of the residents for almost a century thereafter.

This book tells the story of Horwich Works from its inception to its eventual closure in December 1983. The following pages contain many illustrations which serve to confirm the important part played by the Works in both establishing the railway industry and serving the country particularly during the two World Wars.

The Work's siren (buzzer) was a symbol to the generations who spent their working lives at Horwich Works and served as a reliable timepiece for the community as a whole. Its droning tones signalled the beginning and end of working days, it warned workers when their shift was due to start and forewarned families that a particular shift was finishing and the time had arrived to prepare meals and for the children to return home from play. The fire brigade was also summoned to duty by a series of coded signals on the buzzer.

It is sad that all those engineering skills once practised in connection with the manufacture of locomotives have now largely disappeared. Horwich Works not only produced fine engines but more importantly helped to forge the character of individuals. In some ways it moulded the town of Horwich as we know it today.

In an undertaking of this nature, it is not practicable to cover every aspect of the Works in fine detail but it is felt that the contents are sufficient to provide the reader with a reasonable understanding of this extremely interesting part of our local industrial heritage.

Workers leaving Horwich Locomotive Works through the main gates. 1911.

A BRIEF HISTORY OF THE LANCASHIRE
AND YORKSHIRE RAILWAY

A tangle of railways

In August 1837 George Stephenson was appointed Engineer and Consultant for the construction of the Manchester to Leeds Railway. This line had first been discussed twelve years earlier in 1825, and was the beginning of what eventually, through a series of amalgamations, became the Lancashire and Yorkshire Railway. A second railway connection between Manchester and Bolton was opened on the 29th May 1838. Almost three years later, on the 1st March 1841, the longer Manchester to Leeds route was also completed and opened.

Sections of the Manchester to Leeds route had been used before the official opening in 1841. Traffic had run from the terminus at Oldham Road, Manchester, to Littleborough in 1839. In 1844 a second railway station was opened at Hunt's Bank, Manchester, named after the reigning monarch, Victoria.

Amalgamation in 1844 involving the Manchester, Bury and Rossendale Railway and several smaller concerns resulted in a combine which in 1845 became known as the East Lancashire Railway.

The year 1846 saw a further series of mergers between several railway companies. The Manchester to Leeds, Manchester to Bolton, and Liverpool and Bury Railway, (the latter then only one year old) pooled their operations. In 1847 this amalgam was renamed the Lancashire and Yorkshire Railway.

The West Riding Union Railway, the Huddersfield and Sheffield Railway and the Wakefield, Pontefract and Goole Railway were also absorbed into the Lancashire and Yorkshire undertaking in 1847. The East Lancashire Railway was taken over in 1859 and a final merger with the West Lancashire Railway in 1897 completed the rail network of the Lancashire and Yorkshire Railway which girdled England between Liverpool and Goole.

On average, the Lancashire and Yorkshire Railway had a large town every six miles of its track. This made progress relatively slow and led to the nickname the 'Business Line'.

Rolling Stock Maintenance

In considering how best to maintain its rolling stock, the committee and management of the Manchester and Leeds Railway decided to appoint a Locomotive Superintendent. John Todd was elected at a commencing salary of £280 and he started work on the 22nd April 1839, setting up his headquarters at Miles Platting in Manchester. A clash of personalities between Todd and the General Superintendent of the M & L Railway, Captain Laws, led the former to resign his post on the 27th July 1840. He

was replaced by James Fenton who eventually left on the 20th January 1845 to take up an appointment as Acting Engineer on the Leeds and Thirsk Railway.

John Hawkshaw was appointed Chief Engineer of the M & L Railway in 1845. On 3rd February 1845, Hawkshaw proposed William Jenkins as successor to James Fenton. Jenkins was born at Brefi, Cardiganshire, in December 1803. Following his apprenticeship Jenkins worked at Liverpool Docks, and then held a position in charge of cranes and tramroads in the Scottish quarry supplying granite for Liverpool Docks before commencing as an engineer on the Manchester and Bolton Railway in 1835. Prior to his appointment to M & L Railway, Jenkins was responsible for locomotives at the Salford Works of the Manchester and Bolton Railway.

An extension to the Manchester and Leeds Railway network was opened between Miles Platting and Victoria Station, Manchester, on the 1st January 1844. An area of land adjacent to this line locally known as 'Angel Meadow' and situated where John Todd had originally sited his engine shed, was acquired for the construction of a locomotive, carriage and wagon works. Hawkshaw was the designer of the works and they were built by a variety of contractors. On the site were erected the main three storey workshop some 400 feet long and 75 feet wide, engine sheds, boiler shops, stores and a smithy.

As Locomotive Superintendent, Jenkins saw the first locomotive leave the Miles Platting Works in December 1846. The Manchester and Leeds Railway became the first company to build its own engines in its own works. The following year, 1847, saw the M & L Railway amalgamated into the Lancashire and Yorkshire Railway. Jenkins remained at Miles Platting for 22 years but severe restrictions on expenditure meant that locomotives were kept in service for too long and this resulted in extremely poor performances by the company's rolling stock. Failing health caused Jenkins to take sick leave in 1867 and he never resumed work. He died on the 20th November 1867 and was succeeded by William Yates.

A serious fire broke out at the Miles Platting works during the morning of Sunday 27th April 1873, which destroyed almost 10,000 square yards of buildings. The resultant damage was assessed at £55,701. The fire led to the construction of carriage and wagon works at Newton Heath, Manchester, which were intended primarily to relieve the pressure on the Miles Platting Works. Production commenced at the Newton Heath Works during 1877 and they were finally closed in April 1932.

William Barton Wright was appointed Chief Locomotive Superintendent at Miles Platting on the 1st November 1875. He was then almost 47 years old having been born in Northumberland on the 13th November 1828. Following an apprenticeship at the Swindon Locomotive Works and a spell in charge of the Great Western Railway locomotive department at Paddington, London; Barton Wright secured a position as Locomotive and Carriage and Works Superintendent on the Madras Railway, India. John Hawkshaw was Consultant Engineer to the Madras Railway at this time and seems to have influenced Barton Wright's appointment at Miles Platting.

Over the ten year period that Barton Wright was in charge at Miles Platting he replaced nearly all the rolling stock of the Lancashire and Yorkshire Railway employing a policy of the minimum number of standard engines with mostly interchangeable parts.

There was insufficient space at Miles Platting to store properly the number of engines requiring attention and they were packed into the yard awaiting repairs. Residential accommodation and various other buildings surrounded the works thus preventing expansion. The residents of Angel Meadow did not live up to the name and the sight of those engines standing idly in the works yard led to the loss of many of the brass fixtures and fittings by theft. Apparently one locomotive was systematically stripped of all its fixtures, including the boiler, while awaiting repairs.

There was a further small railway manufacturing and repair workshop at Bury which formerly belonged to the East Lancashire Railway and was absorbed into the Lancashire and Yorkshire Railway by amalgamation. The engines built at Bury were of a distinct design with neat outlines, copper capped chimneys and polished brass domes.

Albeit the Lancashire and Yorkshire Railway Company managed to pay its shareholders good dividends, criticism was mounting about their operations and despite having a first class locomotive engineer in Barton Wright he was prevented from realising his full potential due to lack of financial re-investment in the company and the complete inadequacy of the Bury and Miles Platting Works to repair and maintain existing stock, let alone build new replacements. Something had to be done.

John Audley Frederick Aspinall - Beginnings at Crewe

John Audley Frederick Aspinall was born in Liverpool on the 25th August 1851, the second son among the six children of John Bridge Aspinall and Bertha Wyatt Jee. When only 12 years old, John A. F. Aspinall was sent to Beaumont College, Old Windsor, where he displayed no special academic trait but possessed a keen interest in woodwork and things mechanical. By 1867 when he was due to leave college, John A. F. Aspinall had set his mind on becoming a railway engineer and subsequently went to Crewe as a pupil of John Ramsbottom, in December 1867 when aged 17 years and three months.

All pupils were tasked with obtaining practical

John Audley Frederick Aspinall. Chief Mechanical Engineer at Horwich Locomotive Works 1886 - 1899.

experience by working on an engine footplate. In the 1870's railway engines did not have cabs, the only shelter afforded being a weatherboard which provided scant cover on a frosty morning while carrying out shunting work. Generally speaking, pupils worked a 12 hour day from 6.00am to 6.00pm on Monday to Friday and from 10.00am to 12.30pm on Saturdays. In addition, certain studies had to be completed and this rigid schedule left little time for socialising.

John Ramsbottom was President of the Birmingham based Institute of Mechanical Engineers and was responsible for many notable inventions. He was widely respected but failing health forced him to take early retirement in September 1871 when only 57 years of age. His successor, F. W. Webb, had previously worked as Ramsbottom's Chief Assistant and, following favourable reports on Aspinall's ability, Webb used Aspinall as his Indoor Assistant which allowed him to visit America on a fact finding mission to assess the latest advances in railway and steel making. He was then only 20 years old.

During the mid-nineteenth century accommodation was difficult for Crewe apprentices and John A. F. Aspinall along with a fellow student, Henry George Ivatt, rented a house at 168 Hightown, and found someone to cook for them and wash their overalls. The two young men enjoyed hobbies and their home was well equipped with tools including a treadle operated lathe. On trips to see members of his family in the Liverpool area John A. F. Aspinall struck up a friendship with Gertrude Schrader who lived at Camden Lodge, Edge Hill, Liverpool and they were engaged to be married towards the end of 1872.

On completion of his apprenticeship in December 1872, John A. F. Aspinall was appointed by Webb as Indoor Assistant and Manager to the Steel Works at 30 shillings (£1.50p) per week. In due course he hoped that his salary would improve to the point where he could support a wife and family but fate took a hand when his fiancee's mother died in 1874. Her father had died several years previously and her three sisters had all married and left home. She was all alone in the world and Aspinall, with characteristic decisiveness, arranged the wedding for the 2nd September 1874, after which the couple moved to 168 Hightown, Crewe. His companion, Ivatt, had left the address in 1874, when he was posted to Stafford as Assistant Running Shed Foreman.

In January 1875, Webb sent for Aspinall to tell him that he had recommended him for the post of Chief Assistant to the Locomotive Superintendent on the Great Southern and Western Railway and Manager of their works at Inchicore near Dublin. He left Crewe to take up his new duties on the 13th March 1875.

Selection of Horwich as the site for a new locomotive works

Barton Wright was an extremely talented engineer. Since being appointed as Locomotive Superintendent at Miles Platting Works in 1875 he replaced almost all the Lancashire and Yorkshire locomotive stock. There were in the region of 800 engines of over thirty different designs when Barton Wright took office but during his period of tenure these were reduced to five basic standard types with common boilers, cylinders and moving parts.

In August 1882 at a shareholders meeting it was commented that the Management of the Lancashire and Yorkshire Railway Company maintained its unenviable reputation for having the highest rate of working expenses and least dividend of any of the principal railways of England. Shareholders were principally interested in return on their investment which had fallen from 9$\frac{1}{8}$% in 1872 to 5% between 1877 and 1881, which, incidentally, was 2$\frac{1}{2}$% lower than its nearest rival the London and North Western Railway.

At the Annual General Meeting of the Lancashire and Yorkshire Railway Board in 1882 it was resolved that the next Chairman of the Board should also be the Chief Executive Officer and enjoy a generous salary. John Pearson was subsequently appointed to the post and was instrumental in obtaining the services of John Ramsbottom to work in an advisory capacity to the L & Y Railway Board.

It will be remembered that John Ramsbottom was John A. F. Aspinall's mentor while at Crewe and subsequently took early retirement in September 1871 due to failing health. Aspinall eventually left Crewe on the 13th March 1875 to take up a position as Chief Assistant to the Locomotive Superintendent on the Great Southern and Western Railway at Inchicore near Dublin.

Ramsbottom had used his retirement well. His 'Herculean' task at Crewe had left him drained and in poor health but a dozen years of comparative rest had re-vitalised him for a further awesome task. On the 18th of October 1883, Ramsbottom accepted an appointment as Consulting Engineer in matters relating to the Locomotive Department of the Lancashire and Yorkshire Railway.

Soon after taking up the consultancy John Ramsbottom made a detailed examination of the Lancashire and Yorkshire's running sheds and works facilities in the area superintended by Barton Wright. In February 1884, he reported to the Board that the works at Miles Platting and Bury were hopelessly inadequate for the company's needs. The facilities were not sufficient to maintain properly the existing rolling stock let alone build new engines. He added that he felt Barton Wright was pursuing the correct policy in standardising locomotives to four or five types. In short, the Lancashire and Yorkshire Railway needed locomotive workshops on a par with the Crewe Works of the London and North Western Railway.

Ramsbottom and Wright were tasked with finding a suitable site for the construction of a locomotive works. The chief considerations in its selection were the availability and price of labour, a good water supply, cheap coal and a central situation to avoid long runs by light engines.

On the 24th April 1884, reports were submitted on possible sites at Broadfield, Bury, Moston, Castleton, Mirfield, Brighouse, Horbury Junction and a number on the Wakefield-Goole line, but none of them were entirely suitable. Further sites were suggested and examined but, at a meeting held on the 21st May 1884, were also deemed unsatisfactory. At the same meeting, Elias Dorning, Surveyor of the Lancashire and Yorkshire Railway, mentioned that an estate in Horwich was scheduled for auction sale at the Mitre Hotel, Manchester, on the 27th May. Ramsbottom and Wright were interested by Dorning's suggestion and the three men subsequently carried out a survey and were suitably impressed. A special meeting convened for the 26th May received news of the proposal and Dorning was authorised to bid up to £65,000 for the Horwich estate.

Purchase of the Horwich estate

The Horwich estate was auctioned at the Mitre Hotel, Manchester, on the 27th May 1884, by Messrs Lomax, Sons and Mills, and was purchased by the Lancashire and Yorkshire Railway Company.

This view across Horwich dated about 1880 was taken from where the L & Y Railway Company later built a cricket field and recreation ground. Horwich Parish Church can be seen in the centre of the picture.

There are a number of varying accounts as to what acreage the site actually comprised. In his three volume history of the Lancashire and Yorkshire Railway, John Marshall records that 350 acres were secured at a cost of £36,000 (Volume 2, page 209); whilst O. S. Nock in his book 'The Lancashire and Yorkshire Railway - A concise history' refers to a 650 acre site secured at auction for £36,000. (Page 50).

On the 7th June 1884 when the Lancashire and Yorkshire Railway Company released news of the purchase of the Horwich estate it was reported that the company had secured a tract of land covering 379 acres and also the reversion in fee of the freehold estate termed the Wallsuches, Stocks, Makinson Moor and Pilkingtons, containing 357 acres - a grand total of 736 acres at a cost of £36,000; which is just short of £49 per acre.

Development of the site

In early September 1884 the L & Y Railway Company commissioned a lay-out plan for the proposed locomotive works. The area selected for the erection of the new railway works covered 96 acres and lay between Chorley New Road and Red Moss.

The first priority in developing the site was the construction of a branch line from the proposed works complex to join the main rail routes. On the 22nd May 1866 the L & Y Railway Company awarded a contract to Garside and Stead for the construction of a railway line connecting Hindley, Blackrod and Horwich, including a railway station at Horwich. Goods traffic used the line from the 15th July 1868 and passenger traffic from the 14th February 1870. The fork line used to service the locomotive works was eventually completed on the 1st July 1887.

Sharrock's Farm was situated on the site of the proposed locomotive works and in October 1884 the tenant intimated to the L & Y Railway Company that he was anxious to leave. Following a directors' meeting it was decided that the company would take possession of Sharrock's Farm in December 1884. The tenant was eventually paid £200 for what was in effect early possession. By mid December 1884 all the tenants resident on the proposed development site had been served with notice to quit.

In November 1884 Manchester Corporation Waterworks advised the L & Y Railway Company that the Thirlmere Aqueduct would pass through the site of the intended works. Following negotiations between the two parties it was eventually agreed that the aqueduct would be diverted but the extra cost, estimated at £4,600, was to be borne by the railway company.

John Ramsbottom who was a director and consultant for the L & Y Railway Company was largely responsible for the planning and lay-out of Horwich Locomotive works in conjunction with William Barton Wright. A plan of the proposed works and office accommodation was presented to the Board of Directors in November 1884 and in January 1885 it was decided to advertise for tenders for work on the foundations. Joseph D. Nowell submitted a successful tender of £16,129 (less discount) for the foundations of the locomotive erecting shop and work commenced on the 9th March 1885. The eventual cost was £18,179 caused by an error on the drawings which increased the contract price by £2,050.

The various farm buildings which comprised Sharrock's Farm were converted into store rooms and offices for the construction workers. Old Hart's Farm, which also stood on the site earmarked for the works, presented a particular problem in the shape of a very large hill situated near to the farmhouse. Removal of this

Horwich Railway Station. c.1910

eminence required a separate contract so that the ground could be finally levelled to allow construction work. An estimated 450,000 tons of earth required removing and this mammoth task employed 350 men and boys, five locomotives, 130 wagons and two steam driven earthmovers, working night and day for nearly two years. The project was finally completed in October 1886. During this period artificial lighting was rigged to facilitate 24 hour working. Electricity was generated in the farmhouse that was once Sharrock's Farm. On the 12th November 1885, 'Winnie', one of the locomotives used in the clearance of the hill on Old Hart's Farm, rolled over a 60 foot embankment and came to rest on its roof. Fortunately neither the driver nor fireman were hurt.

In May 1885 T. W. Meadows submitted a tender amounting to £42,771 which was accepted by the L & Y Railway Company for the superstructure of the erecting shop and by September that year the work was well underway. Further successful tenders accepted were £12,459 for the construction of the work's offices and £27,540 for building entrances to the works, stores, boiler shops, smithy, forge and foundry - the former tender was sanctioned in September 1885 and the latter in June 1886.

Gas Supply

An ambitious scheme for the locomotive works to produce its own gas supply commenced with the excavation of a reservoir to hold one million gallons of water and the sanction of a tender amounting to £5,200 for the construction of a gasworks near the fork line. Progress on the undertaking was, however, deemed unsatisfactory and, in the event, the L & Y Railway Company contracted with Bolton Corporation to supply gas.

Official Opening

Horwich Locomotive Works was officially opened on the 15th November 1886 and the workforce, many of whom had been transferred from Miles Platting, commenced operations immediately. The first of six locomotives to be repaired was the 'Princess of Wales' built by Messrs Dübs and Company in June 1885. On the 16th July 1885, incidentally, this engine was used when the Prince and Princess of Wales visited the Royal Agricultural Show at Preston.

Completion of Building Works

In the meantime, building work progressed at an astounding rate. A complex system of railway track was laid for transportation about the works. Some 12½ miles of standard gauge railway track and 7½ miles of narrow gauge track were laid. Two miniature railway engines, 'Robin' and 'Wren' were ordered from Beyer Peacock for conveying materials around the works site. these were taken into service on the 7th April 1887. A further

Horwich Locomotive Works, 7th July 1896. This photograph of Horwich Locomotive Works was taken from one of the chimneys and although not particularly clear shows the lines of workshops with Blackrod in the background.

miniature engine 'Dot' was ordered from Beyer Peacock in 1887 and five more - namely 'Fly', 'Wasp', 'Midget', 'Mouse', and 'Bee' - were built at Horwich between 1891 and 1901.

Queen Victoria's Golden Jubilee year (1887) saw the acceptance of tenders for the construction of fitting and paint shops (£12,500), an engine shed (£3,000 approx.), a dining room at Gooch Street and the Mechanic's Institute (£1,627 and £3,140 respectively). In addition, the erection of a steelworks costing £15,000 to £20,000 was agreed by the company. Further building works planned for that year included a millwright's shop (estimated cost £5,893), joiners' shop (£5,241), tin and coppersmiths' shop (£1,690), brass foundry (£1,571), steel foundry (£2,710), signals, points and crossing shop (£5,406), and telegraph department (£1,690).

On the 12th of April 1887 work commenced in the Foundry and on the same day Henry Albert Hoy was transferred from Miles Platting to take up a similar position as Works Manager at Horwich. Hoy was born on the 13th January 1855 and began his apprenticeship at Crewe, under F. W. Webb, in 1872. He was appointed as

Outdoor Assistant to Barton Wright at Miles Platting in 1884 and became Works Manager under J. A. F. Aspinall in 1886.

Extensions to many of the shops were later required. For example, in 1901 the machine shop was extended at a cost of £8,500 and three years later it was necessary to extend the brass foundry. Miles Platting Works were eventually closed in late 1887 with Bury Works closure following a few months later.

Industrial Relations

Industrial relations at Horwich Locomotive Works were generally good but with so many trades being represented and membership of Trade Unions being part of the contract of some employment, there have been occasional strikes and lock-outs.

One particularly nasty dispute involved the English and Irish workmen employed on constructing the Works originally. For some reason the English workmen were paid one halfpenny per hour more than their Irish counterparts which led to much ill-feeling. The situation eventually erupted into violence with running fights in

Labour demonstration outside Horwich Locomotive Works. c.1909.

the streets about Horwich. Bricks, bottles, pokers and a scythe were among the weapons used by the combatants. Order was only restored when a contingent of extra policemen was drafted into the town. A number of those involved in the affray were gaoled without being given the option of a fine.

It was the children who suffered most during strike action because no work meant no pay and therefore no food to eat. During one long running dispute local shopkeepers, including Anyon Kay who had a butchery business on Lee Lane, gave provisions to enable soup kitchens to be set up for the relief of the children of the striking workers.

Despite industrial disputes, which are almost inevitable in such a complex working environment, there remained a loyalty among the workforce and a genuine pride in the locomotives manufactured.

Appointment of John Audley Frederick Aspinall as Chief Mechanical Engineer.

William Barton Wright who, together with John Ramsbottom, had worked so hard to ensure the proper establishment of Horwich Locomotive Works resigned from his post on the 23rd June 1886 to give more time to private practice as an engineer in London. He was then 57 years of age, having been born at North Shields, Northumberland, on the 13th November 1828. He became a director of the Assam Railways and Trading Company Ltd, in India, until 1892 when he returned to London. In 1907 he moved to St. Leonard's-on-Sea, Sussex, where he died on the 7th May 1915.

John Audley Frederick Aspinall, then aged 35 years, was appointed as his successor in July 1886 at a salary of £1,500 per annum. His title was Chief Mechanical Engineer, a new designation adopted by the company.

Aspinall quickly appraised himself of the development taking place at Horwich and also addressed a number of other issues including the provision of accommodation for the workforce and the building of a mechanics' institute funded by a premium apprentice scheme.

Accommodation for the workforce

The census returns for 1881 show Horwich with a population of 3,761 persons comprising 1,799 males and 1,962 females. There were 949 houses of which number 828 were inhabited and one new house was under construction.

When the locomotive works was planned it was envisaged that employment would be provided for 1,300 to 1,400 men. An assessment of available housing in the district revealed 400 unoccupied houses including those standing empty in Horwich. Barton Wright submitted a plan for housing development for the benefit of the workforce suggesting streets with a width of 12 to 16 yards.

Several builders, seeing the opportunity for making a quick profit, constructed properties of a poor standard but to their cost because they did not sell. In 1887 the Bolton Chronicle commented on the housing for the new workforce as follows:-

'Latterly, speculation builders have been very inactive in Horwich, some of them having discovered that the rush to build immediately after the railway started operations was two or three years ahead of time. Several hundred cottages were run up with astonishing rapidity and many of them seem, to the sorrow of both builders and speculators, to be standing empty.'

The Lancashire and Yorkshire Railway Company, further considered the disposal of surplus land in Horwich at a meeting held on the 15th September 1885. It was resolved to reserve sufficient land for a hotel and bowling green and to sell off the remainder for building purposes.

Briefly, the development of the surplus land at Horwich included a road linking Chorley Old Road with Chorley New Road, which was originally intended to be named Jubilee Road but was finally called Victoria Road. A series of 23 streets running parallel to each other was planned between Chorley New Road and the works boundary and a further 15 streets were intended to link Chorley New Road with Victoria Road. Additionally, a complex of streets was proposed to the north of Victoria Road comprising Lesseps Street running parallel with Victoria Road and several short streets to connect Lesseps Street with Victoria Road. A number of large semi-detached properties were built on Victoria Road to serve as residences for heads of departments at the locomotive works; these were known as the 'Villas'.

In recognition of the increased need for religious establishments and business outlets caused by accommodating the workforce a number of plots of land were earmarked specifically for these purposes. The Roman Catholic Bishop of Salford offered a penny a square yard for land on which to build a church in Horwich but this was refused because the company had already requested four pence a square yard for a Wesleyan Chapel.

Victoria Road Wesleyan Chapel. c.1900.

Victoria Road, Horwich. c.1900. Victoria Methodist Chapel and school are on the far left.

Victoria Road, Horwich. c.1900. The trams ran along Victoria Road between 1900 and 1907
and the electricity pylons for the tramway system are visible in the photograph.

Victoria Road, Horwich. 1900.

1882.   VICTORIA CRESCENT, HORWICH.

Victoria Road, Horwich, 1926. In this photograph, taken from the junction with Ramsbottom Road, the road surface is no longer cobbled and the tram poles have been removed. The L & Y Railway Recreation Ground is on the left.

Penn Street, Horwich. c.1902. Penn Street connects Victoria Road with Chorley New Road
and this photograph shows the street from the Chorley New Road end.

Webb Street, Horwich. c.1902.

In the event, only 23 of the 38 streets scheduled for either side of Chorley New Road were built and only Eiffel Street and Nasmyth Street were constructed to the north of Victoria Road. A total of 450 houses were provided in all which was well below the number originally envisaged. Reasons for the reduced requirement for accommodation were that the proposed provision of a wagon works at Horwich, potentially employing up to 1,500 men, never materialised and the private building sector also provided for some of the housing needs for the workforce elsewhere in the town.

Most of the streets constructed, with the obvious exception of Victoria Road, were named after famous engineers. The majority of railway terraces were originally rented out at a cost of between 1/9d to 3/6d per week, with a standard rental of 5/- if piped water and gas were supplied.

Hawkshaw Street, Horwich. c.1902. John Hawkshaw (born 1811) who was one of the most important L & Y Railway engineers, gave name to this street.

HORWICH LOCOMOTIVE WORKS

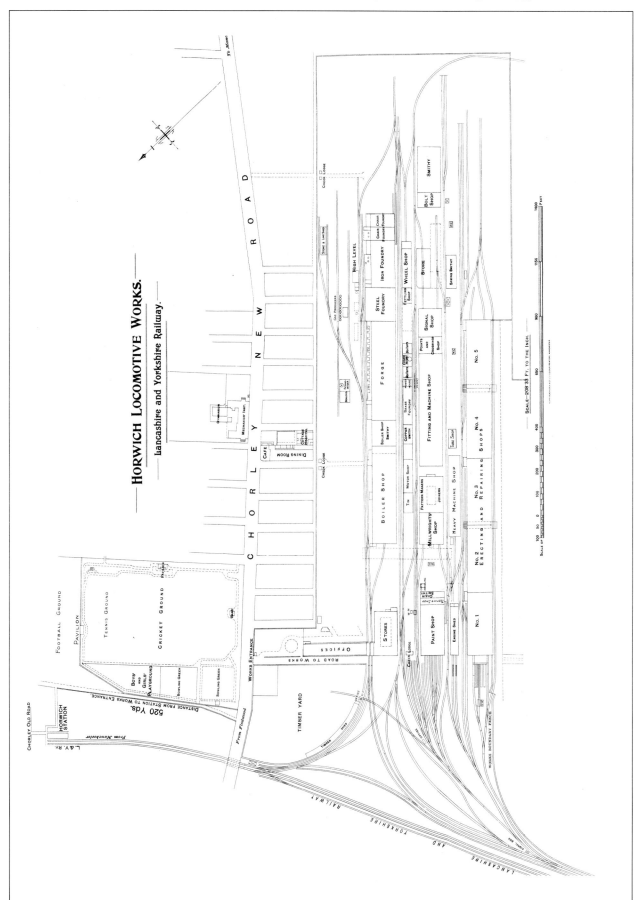

Horwich Locomotive Works. 1911.

Horwich Locomotive Works Yard. c.1905.

Description of the Works

Included below is a description of Horwich Locomotive Works taken from a guide published by the Lancashire and Yorkshire Railway Company in 1911 with additional explanatory material.

These works, of which the building was commenced in 1886, (sic) have been erected for the purpose of repairing and renewing the locomotive stock and of carrying out the mechanical, electrical, and hydraulic engineering work of the railway.

They are situated between Chorley New Road, Horwich, and Red Moss, and are about one mile distant in an easterly direction from Blackrod Station, upon the main line between Manchester and Fleetwood. A fork line has been made, giving direct access to and from Manchester without passing through Blackrod Station.

The land enclosed for the works comprises 116 acres. The covered area of the workshops is 22 acres. They comprise Offices, General Stores, Boiler Shop and Boiler Shop Smithy, Forge, Steel Foundry, Iron and Chair Foundries, Fettling Shop, Bolt Shop and Smithy, Spring Smithy, Signals and Points and Crossing Shops, Fitting and Machine Shops, Boiler and Economiser Houses, Tin and Copper Smiths' Shops, Brass Foundry, Tube Shop, Motor and Telegraph Shops, Millwrights', Joiners', and Pattern Makers' Shops (with gallery for storing patterns), Erecting and Repairing Shops, Engine Shed, Paint Shop, Testing Shop, and Chain Smithy.

For the carriage of materials from the stores and of work to the several shops, 7½ miles of tramway lines have been laid throughout the works, haulage being performed by small locomotives, the cylinders of which are 5 inches diameter by six inches stroke, and the wheels 16 inches diameter. The frames are 7 feet 4 inches overall, and the extreme width of engine is 3 feet. They work at a pressure of 200 lbs per square inch, and their tractive force is about 1,400 lbs., and their weight when full and in working order is 3.57 tons.

Offices

The dimensions of the office accommodation were 323 feet long by 58 feet wide. These were placed at the north-west end of the works, and included a laboratory, fitted up with the requirements for the analysis of all materials. The offices were fitted with electric light, both incandescent and arc lamps, and each department of the works was in telephonic communication with the offices. On either side of a wide corridor, lighted from above, was a series of rooms, some serving as offices, others as private rooms for Mr. Hughes and his chief assistants; while the drawing office was one long, well lighted department accommodating about 16 draughtsmen and tracers. A laboratory, fitted with testing machines and with a chemical section, was also provided. In the drawing office, suspended incandescent lamps were supplemented by reflected illumination from arc lamps shielded from direct vision, the ceiling and walls being painted white to obtain the desired result.

GENERAL VIEW OF HORWICH LOCOMOTIVE WORKS. 1902.

Exterior of Erecting Shop. 1902. The erecting shop comprised five bays and covered an area of 1,520 feet long by 118 feet wide.

Railway engines entered and left the shop on traversers through the large double doors between the compartments. The doors are visible on the right.

Entrance to Horwich Locomotive Works. c.1950. This photograph taken from the practice tower at Horwich Fire Station shows the main administration block incorporating the main entrance.

Horwich Locomotive Works Switchboard. c.1915.

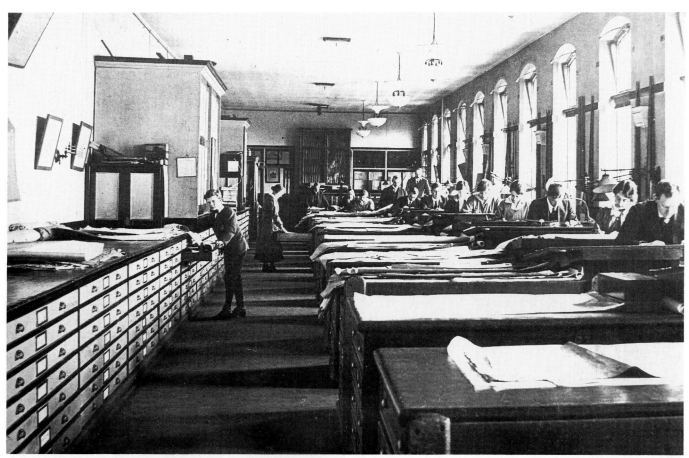

Drawing Office. c.1915.

Mr. Harold Hurst who was a draughtsman at the locomotive works in the early 1920's. He was John McLean's brother-in-law who was librarian at the Mechanics' Institute from 1888 - 1929.

Accounts Office. c.1915.

Alice Gregory is on the left of this photograph taken inside the work's office. c.1915.

Machine Room, work's offices.
c.1915.

Staff Office in the administration building. c.1915.

Office girls. c.1915.

General Stores

Connected directly to the office buildings were the general stores measuring 198 feet long by 111 feet wide, and having a gallery built round the four sides. This building was fitted with the necessary weighing machines, and hydraulic cranes for receiving and storing heavy materials. In line with the stores was the first line of buildings including the boiler shop, boiler shop smithy, forge, steel foundry, iron foundry and chair foundry. Outside the end of the boiler shop the yard was spanned by a long gantry extending into the uncovered area to the left. This gantry was eventually fitted with an electric overhead crane instead of the steam installation previously provided. It served for moving boilers outside the shop as required, and for conveying materials to the right and left of the boiler shop. Another steam crane served the yard between the signal shop and smithy. Transportation between shops was by means of 7½ miles of 18" gauge railway. Some 12½ miles of standard gauge railway also extended throughout the works.

Miniature engine 'Dot' in the wood yard at Horwich. c.1900.

18" GAUGE ENGINE HAULING LOCOMOTIVE BOILER AT HORWICH ENGINE WORKS.

28

Barton Wright 0-6-0 saddletank. This engine, built in June 1877 by Sharp Stewart and rebuilt in the 1890's by Aspinall, was used for shunting operations at Horwich Locomotive Works until its withdrawal in September 1964.

Telegraph Shop

The telegraph shop was 81 feet long by 22 feet wide, fitted with special tools for making and repairing telegraph and block instruments; also automatic screw- making machine, &c. This shop was electrically driven with one motor of 5 horse power.

General view of Telegraph Shop. 1920.

Above: Repairing Telegraph Instruments. Telegraph Shop. 1920.
Below: 4 Spindle Drilling Machine & Semi-automatics. Telegraph Shop. 1920.

Boiler Shop

The boiler shop contained three bays and measured 439 feet long and 111 feet wide. Two bays were reserved for machine tools. The left hand section was mainly reserved for erecting boilers, pits being provided at intervals, so that the boilers could be lowered below ground level to facilitate work on the parts which may be uppermost. The bays were formed by two rows of cast iron columns supporting the longitudinal roof gables. Girders along the outer walls above the side windows form tracks for overhead cranes with shop shafting below, while the roof columns similarly carried girders for the cranes and brackets for shafting. Most of the buildings were arranged more or less on these lines so that detailed reference in each case is unnecessary.

The boiler shop was fitted with a pair of hydraulic pumps and accumulator, two large fixed hydraulic riveters for boiler work, each having hydraulic overhead crane for lifting boilers when riveting; three portable hydraulic riveters on swing frames, bolted to walls and columns; and overhead electrically-driven travelling cranes, in addition to the ordinary machine tools of a boiler shop. Special quadruple multiple stay tapping machine and stay heading machines were provided. Pneumatic caulking and riveting were also in extended use, the furnaces being fired by liquid fuel sprayed on by compressed air. Right-angle plate edge planing machines and multiple drilling machines of different types were in operation. The shop was electrically driven with motors ranging from 5 to 30 Horse Power.

At the end of the Boiler Shop were two Tweddell riveting towers designed by Messrs Fielding and Platt. These would each suspend a standard boiler on end so that the hydraulic riveters could act upon almost any desired part.

North side of Boiler Shop. 1902.

Two views of the Boiler Shop centre bay. 1902.

Above: Boiler Shop looking east. 1902.   *Below:* Boiler Shop south side. 1902.

Hydraulic bending block for angle irons. Boiler Shop Smithy. 1920.

Scrap locomotive boilers stored in the Boiler Shop Yard awaiting cutting up / re-cycling. c.1956.

Another view of scrap boilers awaiting disposal. These two photographs give some idea of the vast tonnage involved in locomotive construction / maintenance and disposal.

0-8-0 engine with boiler fitted.

Scrap boilers outside the Erecting Shop waiting to be scrapped. 1956.

Boiler Shop. c.1910. The size of engine boiler manufactured at Horwich is shown in this interesting photograph.

Boiler Shop Smithy

Adjacent to the boiler shop was the boiler shop smithy, 120 feet long by 111 feet wide, fitted with the usual smiths' fires and a gas furnace on either side for heating the blanks. Also fitted were hydraulic flanging presses for flanging firebox backs, tube plates, throat plates, ashpans, tank splasher plates, &c. This shop was electrically driven with motors of 20 and 60 Horse Power.

Boiler Shop Smithy flanging press. 1902.

Forge

Beyond the boiler shop smithy was the forge some 452 feet long by 111 feet wide, which contained Siemens' regenerative furnaces for re-heating, the doors of which were pneumatically raised; an annealing furnace, a 14-inch merchant mill and a 8½-inch guide mill, together with tyre mill and a 30-inch cogging mill with electrically driven live rolls; a 35-ton duplex hammer, and one 8-ton and two 5-ton hammers. 16 gas producers of Wilson type supply gas to all the forge furnaces.

Scrap for billets was cut up on the high level by powerful shearing machines, and was passed from these by a hopper to a long barrel, which acted as a scrap cleaner and a conveyor to the scrap benches.

Above: Forge - 70 cwts hammers. 1902.
Below: Forge - Cogging mill. 1902.

Above: Forge - Bar rolling mill. 1902.   *Below:* Forge - Tyre rolling mill. 1902.

Above: Fish plate plant forge. 1920.

Below: Tyre rolling mill & engine forge. 1920.

Rolling bar iron guide mill forge. 1920.

Steel Foundry. c.1890.

Steel Foundry

The steel foundry extended 150 feet long by 135 feet wide, and was fitted with "Siemens-Martin" regenerative melting furnaces, having high level tramway for carrying ladle, electrically driven with 7 Horse Power motor, and narrow gauge tramway beneath for mould trollies, also core drying furnaces, moulding machines, &c. The whole of the furances in the steel foundry were heated by gas made from 9 Wilson's gas producers. The "Tropenas" process for making steel castings was also in operation.

Above: Steel Foundry.1902.
Below: Casting steel carriage wheel from stopper ladle (Tropenas steel). Steel Foundry. 1920.

Above: Steel Foundry looking east. 1902.

Below: Steel Foundry - Tropenas converters

Iron Foundry

The Iron Foundry was served by two cupolas and four revolving moulding machines or 'roundabouts' were installed. Dimensions of the Iron Foundry were 212 feet long by 111 feet wide and hydraulic power was used for working the cranes. In addition there were overhead (electrically-driven) travelling cranes, which could be used in both Steel and Iron Foundries.

The natural formation of land, which necessitated the rail level at the rear end of foundries being considerably higher than the floors of foundries, permitted of coke and iron being unloaded and wheeled direct to the charge holes of the cupolas or the melting furnaces. Similarly, the gas producers for the furnaces were charged direct at the top, whilst the ashes from producers were drawn out at the bottom into the tram wagons running on the lower level. There were two motors in this shop, each of 3 and 18 Horse Power.

Iron Foundry looking east. 1902.

Above: Axlebox moulding machines & turntables. Iron Foundry. 1920.

Below: Group of core makers. Iron Foundry. 1920.

Cylinder moulding. Iron Foundry. 1920.

Chair and Plate Foundry

Measuring 124 feet long by 128 feet wide, the chair and plate foundry was similarly fitted with two cupolas charged from the high level. Hydraulic charging arrangements were used in connection with these cupolas. A Staging was provided for fettling the chairs, which were then placed on an endless chain, which conveyed them to the railway wagons for despatch. Siemens-Martin regenerative smelting furnaces were arranged at one side of the steel foundry and supplied with gas from nine Wilson producers.

As regards wheels, centres up to 5' 9" in diameter were made this way, so that it was only 7' 3" engine wheels which had to be moulded elsewhere. Machine moulding was largely adopted and was practised for nearly all repetition work. To the left of this range of buildings, reckoning from the offices, the ground rises towards the chair foundry and this fact was utilised to allow coke and iron to be unloaded and wheeled directly to the charge holes of the cupolas and furnaces.

Dressing castings in the Fettling Shop. c.1900.

Chair Foundry. 1902.

Fettling Shop. 1902.

Carriage and Wagon Wheel Shop

Dimensions of this shop were 200 feet long by 47 feet wide, fitted with lathes for boring and turning carriage and wagon wheels; also a hydraulic press for pressing the tyres on the wheels, and a press for forcing the wheels on the axles. There was also a special multiple drill for drilling holes in the retaining rings, wood blocks, and steel wheels, at one setting. Pneumatic tools were applied to the dressing of steel castings. This shop was fitted with shafting on either side which was entirely electrically driven with motors of 20 and 30 Horse mounted overhead.

Above: Wheel Shop. 1902.

Below: General view of Wheel Shop. 1920.

Views of Wheel Shop showing manufacture of rolls and straight axles. 1920.

Smithy Bolt Shop

Extending over an area of 60 feet long by 111 feet wide, this shop contained various bolt and nut making machines, drop stamps, three "Rollo" 12 cwt., one steam 5 cwt.; a large Ajax forging machine, and several Bradley hammers were in operation, the furnaces in the shop being heated in some cases with liquid fuel and others with coke.

Smithy

The smithy covered an area of 212 feet long by 111 feet wide, and was provided with 11 double and 26 single hearths, also nine steam hammers, &c., and fitted with "Roots" blower for the blast; 8 drop stamps (three 20 cwt., one 30 cwt., these being steam stamps, the remaining four, 12 cwt., being "Rollo" pattern). This shop was electrically driven with motors ranging from 5 to 80 Horse Power.

Smithy - north side. 1902.

Above: Smithy - south side. 1902.   *Below:* View of south bay - General Smithy. 1920.

Two "Bradley" hammers (200 lbs) used for swaging & piecing-up rods, levers, shafts etc. - General Smithy. 1920.

View of steam drop hammers for stampings - General Smithy. 1920.

Spring Smithy

This shop was 153 feet long by 47 feet wide, fitted with three gas-heated spring furnaces, hydraulic spring buckle press, also buckle stripping machine and steam hammer.

Special self-contained plant for making spring plates, comprising electrically-driven punching, nibbing, and shearing machines.

Spring Smithy. 1902.

Above: General view of Spring Smithy showing testing of spring in left foreground. 1920.

Below: Nibbing and slotting machines - Spring Smithy. 1920.

Signal Shop

Standing in the same row of shops as the bolt shop smithy and smithy, the signal shop was 128 feet long by 111 feet wide, and was used for fitting up all locking frames and general signal work, a rack-saw being provided for signal posts, boring machine and other special tools. This shop is in part electrically driven by two motors of 5 and 18 Horse power. A steam crane served the yard between the signal shop and smithy.

Signal Shop - north side. 1902

Signal Shop - south side. 1902.

Signal frame in course of erection - Signal Shop. 1920.

Points and Crossing Shop

Standing between the fitting and machine shop, and the signal shop; the points and crossing shop was 72 feet long by 111 feet wide, provided with special machinery for dealing with the manufacture of points and crossings, and included angular planing machines, Duplex slotting machine, and special machine for milling and drilling locking frame standards at one setting.

General views of Points and Crossings Shop. 1920.

Fitting Shop

The fitting shop comprised 3 bays and measured 508 feet long by 111 feet wide. It was fitted up with a large number of milling and other machines for dealing with locomotive work, including several automatic machines and turret lathes for turning copper firebox stays, bolts, pins, &c.; also drilling and slotting machines. On entering the shop from the pattern makers' department three enclosures existed. A Holroyd screw and worm milling machine was used specially for making the reversing screws of locomotives. These machines were driven by wall engines bolted at the end of the shop, giving motion by means of bevel gearing to four ranges of shafting running longitudinally. Four 5-ton high-speed electrically-driven jib travelling cranes controlled the machines on each side. The machines in this shop were in part electrically driven by 14 motors, ranging from $1\frac{1}{2}$ to 20 Horse Power.

Fitting Shop - centre bay. 1902.

Above: Fitting Shop - centre bay looking west. 1902.
Below: Fitting Shop - centre bay looking east. 1902.

Above: Fitting Shop - centre bay looking west. 1902.

Below: Fitting Shop tool room. 1902.

Above: Group of drilling machines - Machine Shop. 1920.

Below: Turret lathes for brass work - Machine Shop. 1920.

Above: Group of planing machines - Machine Shop. 1920.

Below: Group of shaping machines - Machine Shop. 1920.

Above: Universal milling machine gasking wheel for electric capstan in foreground.
Tool Room - Machine Shop. 1920.

Below: Group of semi-automatics with gear-cutting machine in foreground. 1920.

Above: Group of slotting machines - Machine Shop. 1920.

Below: Group of milling machines with slab milling machine in foreground - Machine Shop. 1920.

Above: New motion bench with marking-out bench in foreground - Machine Shop. 1920.

Below: Groups of automatics used in the manufacture of bolts, pins, studs, etc. - Machine Shop. 1920.

Above: Grinding milling cutters - Tool Room, Machine Shop. 1920.

Below: Group of vertical milling machines - Machine Shop. 1920.

Motor driven five-ton walking jib crane in the machine shop.

Boiler House (High and Low Level)

Each containing a battery of Lancashire boilers, some fitted with underfeed mechanical stokers and "Green's" economiser, others with forced draught grates for burning inferior fuel.

Horwich Locomotive Works Boiler House. c.1920.

The boiler house chimney was demolished during the 1960's and it was necessary to dismantle it brick by brick because of surrounding buildings.

71

Boiler House. c.1955.

Central Power Station

Covering an area of 32 feet long by 47 feet wide, this shop was equipped with one 800 K.W. horizontal mixed-pressure British Thompson-Houston Curtis turbo alternator set, working in conjunction with a 750 K.W. rotary converter supplying current at 250 volts, two 300 K.W. Bellis and Morcom high-speed engines and dynamos, and two small 60 K.W. sets. Practically the whole of the works were supplied for power and lighting purposes by this plant. In connection with the power station there was a barometric condenser (Mirlees Watson type), which dealt with the steam from several other engines of large capacity - thus forming a central condensing plant.

Above: Interior of Power House No. 2. at Horwich Locomotive Works. c.1902.

Left: Arthur Jones pictured in the works power house. c.1920.

Brass Foundry

The brass foundry extended 164 feet long by 47 feet wide, and was fitted with gas furnaces for melting heavy work, crucible furnaces being coke fired, special core-drying stove, heated with waste gases from crucible furnaces

Brass Foundry. 1902.

Morgan's tilting furnaces - Brass Foundry. 1920.

Coppersmiths' Shop

Standing next to the brass foundry was the coppersmiths' shop some 89 feet long by 47 feet wide, fitted with the necessary appliances for dealing with all tin and copper work used on the railway.

Copper Shop. 1902.

Above: Copper Shop. 1902.

Below: General view of Copper Shop. 1920.

Tube Shop

Measurements of the tube shop were 82 feet long by 35 feet wide. It was fitted up with a complete tube cleaning and repairing plant, electrically driven by 20 Horse Power motor. Equipment in the shop included rattlers for tube cleaning, 3-ton overhead electric runway for conveying tubes to rattlers, acetylene generator for "pit" welding, cutting off, end boring, &c., machines, and brazing hearths.

General view of Tube Repairing Shop. 1920.

Motor Shop

Adjoining the coppersmiths' shop was the motor shop 153 feet long by 47 feet wide, used for making and repairing motors and their accessories. This shop was electrically driven by 9 motors, ranging from 3 to 5 Horse Power.

Motor Shop. 1895. Inside the motor shop prior to the balcony being constructed.

Motor Shop. 1902.

General view of Motor Shop. 1920.

Electrical motor test bed - Motor Shop. 1920.

Tinsmiths' Shop

Next to the Motor Shop was the Tinsmiths' Shop some 92 feet long by 47 feet wide, arranged with tin-making plant for dealing with railway requirements. The machines in this shop were electrically driven, partly from the motor shop, and with one 7 Horse Power motor fixed in the shop.

Tinsmiths' Shop. 1895. This view of the tinsmiths' shop was taken before the balcony was fitted.

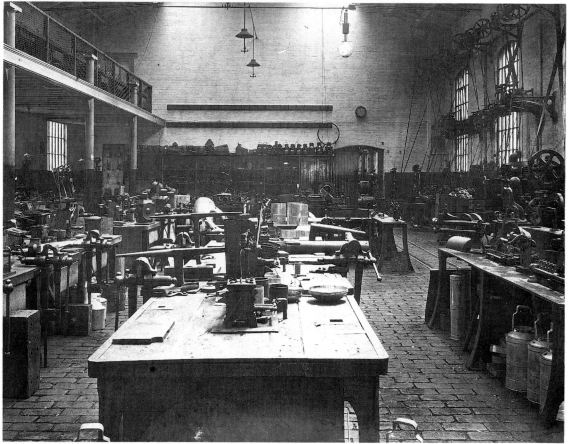

Tinsmiths' Shop. 1902.

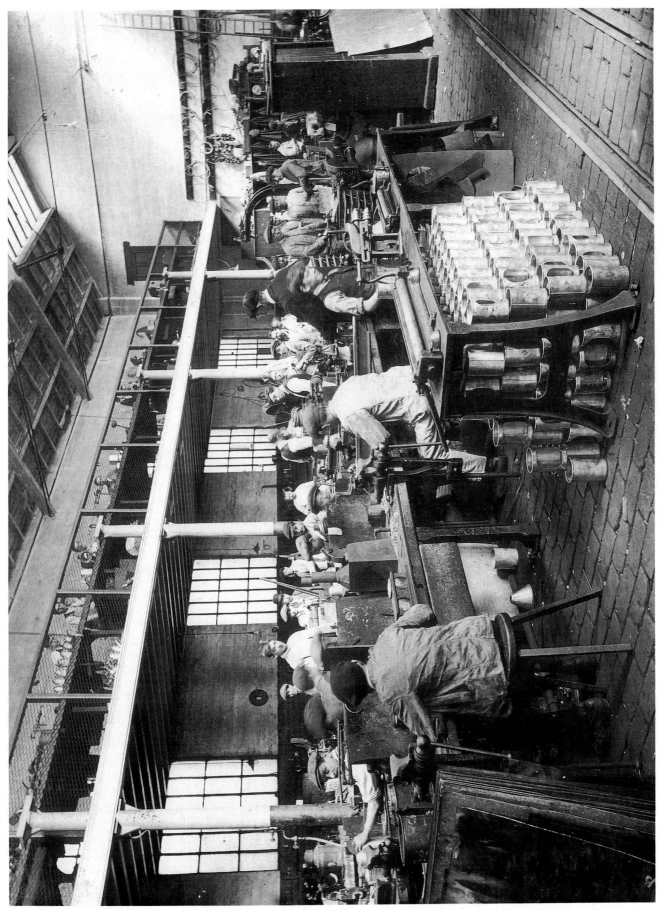

General view of Tin Shop. 1920.

Joiners' and Pattern Makers' Shop

This shop was 164 feet long by 111 feet wide, and was fitted up with modern machinery for sawing, boring, morticing, &c., including a special pattern making machine by Wadkin & Co., of Leicester which enabled many of the less straight forward shaping operations to be easily and accurately effected. This shop was electrically driven, the motors being 10 and 40 Horse. A gallery was carried round the shop for storing patterns. A sprinkler arrangement was fitted in this shop in case of fire.

Pattern Makers' and Joiners' Shop - Pattern side. 1902.

Belt repairing etc. Joiners' Shop. 1920.

General view of Joiners' Shop. 1920.

General view of Pattern Shop. 1920.

Millwrights' Shop

In this shop extending 143 feet long by 111 feet wide all the hydraulic and general repairing work for the line was carried out. There were three overhead travelling cranes electrically operated, and this shop was driven electrically; the motors being three 10 and one 20 Horse, and other special machinery for the work required.

Millwrights' Shop. 1902.

Opposite, above: Boring, milling & facing machine - Millwrights' Shop. 1920.

Opposite, Below: "Asquith" radial arm drilling machine, drilling 200 H.P. motor carcase - Millwrights' Shop. 1920.

Heavy Machine Shop

This long, relatively narrow shop, measured 360 feet long by 48 feet wide and was fitted with frame plate straightening, slotting, and radial arm drilling machines; also crank pin boring, keyway milling, and slotting machines; also special plant for manufacture of built-up crank axles, crank, straight axle, and large wheel lathes.

Many of the machines in this shop were specially constructed for the purposes required, and all machines were individually driven by 3-phase alternating current motors.

Two 10-ton 3-motor electrically-driven overhead travelling cranes controlled the machines on each side.

Two views of Heavy Machine Shop. 1902.

Engine frame plate slotting machine - Heavy Machine Shop. 1920.

Turning crank axle & boring crank web - Heavy Machine Shop. 1920.

Tyre heating furnace. Men in act of lowering wheel into tyre - Heavy Machine Shop. 1920.

Erecting Shop

The gigantic erecting shop was divided into 5 bays and extended over an area of 1,520 feet long by 118 feet wide. This shop was arranged for the repair of existing and the building of new engines and tenders, and was provided with twenty 30-ton electrically-driven overhead travelling cranes, portable hydraulic riveters, flexible shaft drilling machines driven by motors, and the necessary tools for repairs. Access for engines to the centre portion of this long shop was obtained by two electrically-driven traversers. Wheel lathes, in some cases electrically-driven, were provided in various positions for conveniently dealing with wheels taken from engines under repair.

Above: Erecting Shop No. 1. 1902

Right: Erecting Shop No. 2. centre bay. 1902.

General view of Erecting Shop. 1902.

Above: Erecting Shop No. 4. 1902.
Below: Erecting Shop No. 5. 1902.

Erecting Shop. 1902.

Erecting Shop. 1902.

Wheeling a locomotive - Erecting Shop. 1920.

Above: New locomotive in course of erection - Erecting Shop. 1920.

Below: Fitting boiler mountings - Erecting Shop. 1920.

Above: Repairing locomotives - Erecting Shop. 1920.

Below: Erecting Shop. c.1910. This excellent photograph of 2-4-2 Tank Engine No. 675 suspended by chains from one of the overhead cranes in the erecting shop gives some idea of the handling capabilities at Horwich Locomotive Works to build and repair engines.

Paint Shop

Measuring 234 feet long by 111 feet wide, this shop, unlike all the other shops, had a weaving shed type of roof, therefore obtaining a light free from sun glare. It was steam heated and fitted with the necessary grinding and mixing machines, which were electrically driven by one 3 Horse Power motor, and provided with heating arrangement for the thorough drying of the paint quickly.

Painting engines - Paint Shop. 1920.

Paint mixing machines - Paint Shop. 1920.

Test Shop and Chain Smithy

The test shop was 111 feet long by 27 feet wide, and the chain smithy 111 feet long by 28 feet wide. These shops were fitted with a 100-ton hydraulic testing machine; also oil, spring, and 100-ton hydraulic chain-testing machines all of Wicksteed design, constructed by Buckton & Co., of Leeds. All chains were tested before being sent out for use. There were also steam hammers, and the necessary machines for finishing test specimens, the machines being electrically driven by one 7 Horse Power motor. Outside the smithy was a chain annealing furnace.

Above: Test Room. 1902.

Left: General view of Test Room. 1920.

Above: General view of Test Room. 1920.
Below: General view of Chain Smithy. 1920.

Gas Works

These were situated on the south-west boundary of the works, and at a much lower level. They were of sufficient capacity to light all the company's workshops and premises at Horwich and Blackrod, although a greater part of the works were eventually lit by electricity.

Dining Rooms

These were erected near the public entrance to the works for the accommodation of the men who lived at a distance. Accommodation was provided for 1,100 men, whose meals were cooked or heated by attendants in charge of the rooms.

The Dining Room is the low roofed building standing to the rear of the L & Y Arms Cafe. c.1902.

Interior of L & Y Railway Co. Dining Room, Horwich. c.1902.

LOCOMOTIVES DESIGNED AND BUILT AT HORWICH

William Barton Wright was appointed by the L & Y Railway Company as Chief Locomotive Superintendent at their Miles Platting works on the 1st November 1875 and took over his duties in 1876. He was appalled by the standard of engines possessed by the company and is reported to have ordered the scrapping of twelve engines at one Lancashire shed in the first month. A contemporary railway enthusiast, Mr. E. L. Ahrons, who spent much of his time in the Leeds - Bradford area, was later to describe the situation on the L & Y Railway at that time in a series of articles published in the Railway magazine from 1915 onwards, as follows:- " A railway of ugly inconvenient stations, of old broken down engines and dirty carriages, and of a superlative unpunctuality, to which no pen could do justice".

During his ten years at Miles Platting, Barton Wright vigorously pursued a policy of standardisation and was responsible for providing the L & Y Railway Company with a stock of strong, simple and efficient locomotives which did much to improve the image of the company. Despite this, the L & Y Railway Board were reluctant to commit heavy capital expenditure on improvements at the Miles Platting works and, as a result, no more than 40 of Barton Wright's 0-6-0 engines were built there between 1876 and 1880.

Many engines designed by Barton Wright had to be supplied by outside contractors which relieved the pressure at Miles Platting but added to the difficulties in ensuring that the designs were properly and correctly interpreted. Among the companies who supplied engines to Barton Wright's designs were Kitsons, Neilson & Company, Sharp Stewart, Dübs and the Vulcan Foundry.

It was mainly due to Barton Wright's persistence in urging the L & Y Railway Board to improve workshop facilities that the Chairman of the company, John Pearson, appointed John Ramsbottom as a consultant engineer to assess the company's needs. The outcome was the construction of Horwich Locomotive Works.

John Audley Frederick Aspinall was appointed Chief Mechanical Engineer at Horwich Locomotive Works following Barton Wright's resignation on the 23rd June 1886. Apart from problems associated with the works which were then nearing completion, the L & Y Railway Company was desperately short of engines. Aspinall recommended that the stock of existing engines should be increased from 963 to 1,114 and in addition a further 13 engines were required to operate the new Liverpool line then under construction; making a grand total of 164 engines.

As an emergency measure Aspinall was authorised to order twenty 0-6-0s and sixteen 4-4-0s from the Vulcan Foundry. A further thirty 0-6-0s and thirty 4-4-0s were ordered from Beyer Peacock & Co., along with two miniature engines 'Wren' and 'Robin'. The thirty 4-4-0s built by Beyer Peacock were of a slightly modified design incorporating the Neilson engines with Joy valve gear. They were numbered from 978 to 1007. A third miniature engine 'Dot', was subsequently ordered from Beyer Peacock in November 1887.

4-4-0 Beyer Peacock 6' 0" passenger engine No. 10109 in early L.M.S. livery following a re-build at Horwich Locomotive Works. It was originally entered in service during September 1888 bearing No. 985 and was one of the last batch of 30 such engines built by Beyer Peacock before Horwich Locomotive Works opened. The engine remained in service until October 1932.

0-4-0T, 18 inch gauge engine 'Wren'. In order to move materials around the Horwich Locomotive Works site, John A. F. Aspinall ordered two 0-4-0 tank engines from Beyer Peacock at £250 each which were delivered on the 7th April 1887 and named 'Wren' and 'Robin'. A third Beyer Peacock engine 'Dot' was ordered on the 8th November 1887 and cost £300. The engine named 'Wren' is shown in the photograph. Five other miniature engines namely 'Fly', 'Wasp', 'Midget', 'Mouse' and 'Bee' were subsequently built at Horwich Locomotive Works.

When the works at Horwich were opened in November 1886 the L & Y Railway Company possessed 1,000 engines comprising 353 passenger-engines and 647 goods-engines. There were 29 different types of passenger-engines and 26 types of goods-engines. Aspinall resolved to reduce these numbers and produce standardisation and, wherever possible, interchangeability of parts.

The engines of the Lancashire and Yorkshire Railway were painted dark green, with black bands and white lining until 1876 when Barton Wright took over and had all engines painted black without lining. From 1878 the colour of all new engines was changed from black to light green and finally, in 1883 the familiar black with red and white lining became the L & Y Railway Company livery. Engine number-plates were painted in the colour of the maker, vermilion for engines built at Miles Platting, green for those built by Beyer Peacock & Co., blue for Kitsons, &. etc. With the exception of the miniature gauge engines, none of the L & Y stock was named. Aspinall apparently had an aversion to this practice and if an engine was received with a name-plate it was quickly removed.

When Horwich Locomotive Works was initially opened six locomotives were taken in for repair. The first engine to be built at Horwich was an Aspinall 2-4-2 standard radial passenger tank engine which left the works on the 20th February 1889 bearing the number 1008. This was a continuance on the numbering used in the batch of thirty 4-4-0s built by Beyer Peacock & Co., between July 1888 and April 1889. From 1889 all new locomotives were built at Horwich.

A great variety of engines were designed and built at Horwich Locomotive Works. There is some controversy as to which engine can rightly be claimed to have been the 'thousandth' built. The Locomotive Magazine for August 1907 bestows the distinction on an 0-8-0 coal engine No. 1471 while the engine which carries the works No. 1000 is an 0-8-0 engine No. 1497. It is agreed that neither of these two engines was the thousandth but the distinction correctly belongs to an 0-4-0 railmotor, Engine No. 15, works No. 983. The reason for the discrepancy is that the first seventeen 0-4-0 saddle tank engines, known as 'Pugs', built at Horwich were not allocated works (or progressive) numbers.

0-4-0 Railmotor carrying L.M.S. No. 10612 at Horwich Railway Station.
This engine was L & Y Works No. 983 - the thousandth engine built at Horwich Locomotive Works.

In an address to the Institution of Mechanical Engineers at Liverpool in July 1909, George Hughes, C.M.E. at Horwich Locomotive Works, presented a paper entitled 'Locomotives designed and built at Horwich with some results'. At that time the L & Y Railway Company possessed 1,517 locomotives; 1,052 of which had been constructed at Horwich.

The L & Y Railway Company amalgamated with the London & North Western Railway Company on 1st January 1922. A merger of the two companies had been under discussion since 1871 and a number of agreements were already in place before the merger which allowed the separate companies to operate fairly closely. The L & Y Railway became Division B of the L & N W Railway. This merger was only in existence for twelve months because the L & N W Railway was itself absorbed into a grouping of railway companies to become part of the London Midland and Scottish Railway network on 1st January 1923. (It is relevant to mention these mergers because many of the railway engines built at Horwich were allocated different numbers following the mergers). The railways of Britain were nationalised on the 1st January 1948.

George Hughes remained as C. M. E. at Horwich during the period in which the above mentioned mergers took place. The sad result of these mergers as far as Horwich Locomotive Works was concerned was that the power base was shifted from Horwich to the locomotive works at Derby. This fact contributed to George Hughes taking early retirement in 1925 at 60 years of age.

After the second world war a whole series of events combined to diminish the importance of Horwich Locomotive Works. Diesel powered trains and electrification schemes gradually phased out the need for steam locomotives. The 'Beeching Report' on British Rail (1963) proposed a number of improvements designed to reshape British Railways to suit modern conditions. The thought underlying the whole Report was that railways should be used to meet that part of the total transport requirement of the country for which they offered the best available means, and that they should cease to do things for which they are ill suited. Among the recommendations were the discontinuance of many stopping passenger services, closure of a high proportion of the total number of small stations to passenger traffic, reduction of the uneconomic freight traffic through small stations by closing them progressively, rapid progressive withdrawal of freight wagons and continued replacement of steam by diesel locomotives. The last steam locomotive (No. 76099) left the works on 27th November

1957 after which a programme was introduced for the manufacture of shunting diesels. This type of work was carried out until the end of 1962 during which time 169 diesel locomotives were constructed. Operations at Horwich were then reduced to the repair of engines. The last steam locomotive to be repaired at Horwich Locomotive Works was a Stanier 8F No. 48756 which left the works on the 8th of May 1964. The only responsibility which finally remained was the maintenance of railway wagons.

Horwich Locomotive Works operated from November 1886 when the first six locomotives were taken in for repair until its closure in 1983, a total of 97 years. Altogether, 1,830 steam locomotives and five 18" gauge locomotives were built. In addition some 50,000 locomotives were repaired over the first 76 year period.

The first locomotive to be built at Horwich

The Aspinall 2-4-2 Radial Tank locomotive No. 1008 was the first locomotive manufactured at Horwich Locomotive Works in a batch of ten begun in January 1888. All the parts were made at Horwich except the wheels and tyres which were obtained from Germany because the steel foundry at Horwich was not then in production. It left the works on 20th February 1889 and was taken into service at Southport. John Audley Frederick Aspinall designed this locomotive which incorporated a two way vacuum operated water scoop to allow for a much greater water capacity. The locomotive worked the Midland services in 1926 under the L.M.S. number 10621 and was discharged from duty on 18th September 1954, bearing British Rail No. 50621. The engine was granted a preservation order as an item of historical interest and was eventually refurbished at Horwich Works leaving on 7th September 1964. It was not possible to obtain all the parts necessary to restore the engine for 'running' and a number of components, including the chimney, were made from timber to the design of Mr. Geoffrey Drinkwater, the chief draughtsman.

Engine No. 1008 can be seen centre foreground in Lancashire & Yorkshire livery after being refurbished at Horwich in 1964. Initially the engine went to Stratford Works but it was transferred to be stored at Preston Park, Brighton, on the 19th February 1968. With the closure of Preston Park storage depot the engine was removed to Birmingham Steam Museum and finally arrived at the National Railway Museum in York on the 23rd June 1976.

2-4-2 Radial Tank Engine No. 1042. Engine No. 1042 (in photograph) left the works on the 11th July 1890 and was eventually withdrawn from service on the 7th May 1952. Nearly every L & Y Railway Shed had an allocation of these engines which remained in regular production until 1911.

2-4-2 Tank Engine No. 227. This engine entered service on the 26th May 1911 incorporating a combination of Belpaire boilers and Schmidt superheaters. It was the final development of Aspinall's original 2-4-2 design.

A Miscellany of Horwich locomotives.

Aspinall's 4-4-2 "1400" Class Express engine - L.M.S. No. 10327. When this type of engine first left Horwich Works on 22nd February 1899, it was the most powerful in existence on a British railway. Aspinall had successfully argued that the high centre of gravity made the engine more stable. This engine stayed in service until 22 November 1929.

4-4-0 Passenger engine No. 1099 facing 4-4-2 Express engine No. 1400. Passenger engine No. 1099 was built at Horwich in July 1891 and the express engine No. 1400 was completed on the 23rd February 1899. Demands for an express train led to the production of the 4-4-2 (shown right) which was designed from the 4-4-0 (facing it). The engine No. 1400 had the largest boiler on any British locomotive at that time with the exception of the North Eastern Railway 7ft. 6in. 4-4-0s Nos. 1869 and 1870.

L.M.S. 0-6-0 Goods Engine No. 12151. Originally built in 1892 with the L & Y No. 1136, this engine was in service as the Mirfield, West Yorkshire, breakdown train. It was withdrawn on the 28th May 1932.

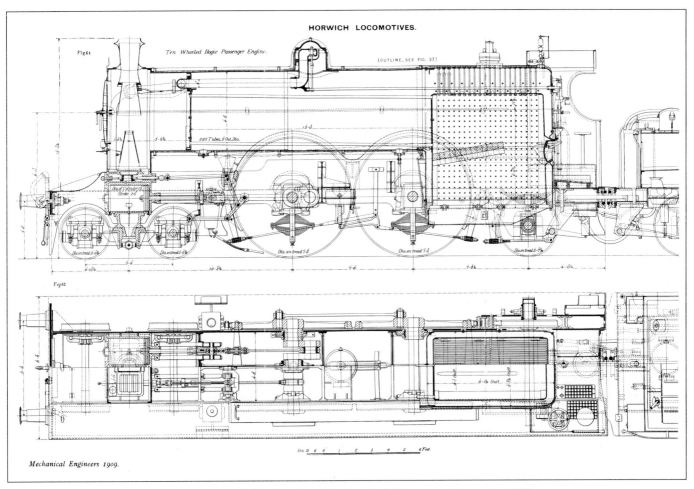

Ten Wheeled Bogie Passenger Engine.

(OUTLINE, SEE FIG. 27.)

Fig 61

225 Tubes, 2 Out.Dia.

Fig 62

Mechanical Engineers 1909.

Diagram of 4-4-2 Engine from Mechanical Engineers Magazine 1909.

Technical data
Cylinders - Diameter 19", Stroke 26"
Wheels - Bogie 3' 0$^{1}/_{2}$"
Coupled 7' 3"
Trailing 3' 7$^{3}/_{4}$"
Boiler -   Diameter 4' 10"
Length 15' 0"
Firebox Shell - 8' 1" long and 4' 1" wide.
Copperbox - 7' 5 and five eighths" long and 6' 11$^{1}/_{2}$"
high.
Tubes - 225 x 2" outside diameter.
Heating surface - 1,767 tubes - Firebox 161' 0"
Firegrate - 23' 0"
Tank capacity - 2,290 gallons.

0-6-0 Goods Engine No. 417. Built to Aspinall's design, Engine No. 417 went into traffic on the 16th September 1895. Between the 12th September 1889 and May 1901 some 400 similar engines were built at Horwich. The engine shown was withdrawn on the 21st May 1938.

L & Y Engine No. 1, Hughes re-build of a standard Aspinall 0-6-0 with a Belpaire boiler and a Schmidt superheater added in November 1913. The engine entered service on the 15th September 1896 and was withdrawn on the 29th September 1951.

2-4-2 Tank Engine No. 1375. Built at Horwich and entering service on the 29th April 1898, this engine was fitted with Druitt Halpin thermal storage apparatus and had a short bunker. The thermal storage apparatus was largely unsuccessful and was eventually removed. The locomotive remained in service until December 1933.

0-8-0 Coal Engine No. 65 with Aspinall Boilers. The need to tranship coal from Goole to Liverpool resulted in Aspinall's last design of a powerful 0-8-0 engine. Construction began in November 1889 and No. 65 left the works on the 14th July 1902. This engine was withdrawn in April 1927.

Below: 0-4-0 Railmotor Engine No.6. Several railway companies experimented with steam railmotors to reduce running costs and George Hughes, C.M.E. at Horwich, had a design prepared at Horwich in 1905. Eighteen such engines were built at Horwich between 1906 and 1911. Engine No. 6 was withdrawn from service in May 1927. The photograph was taken at Ormskirk Engine Shed.

0-8-0 Coal Engine No. 1472. George Hughes, C.M.E. at Horwich carried out experiments on modified Aspinall 0-8-0s and showed that it was possible to effect a 25% saving in coal consumption. In 1906 he was authorised to build 20 compound 0-8-0s. Only 10 were in effect built, Nos. 1471 - 1480, between April and June 1907. Engine No. 1472 (pictured) was withdrawn from service in September 1926.

4-6-0 Unsuperheated 4 Cylinder Engine No. 1508. Designed in 1907 by George Hughes, this engine entered service on the 17th July 1908. It was designed without superheaters and incorporated slide valves and Joy's gear. The engine operated under L.M.S. No. 10401 and was withdrawn from service in January 1926.

0-8-2 Banking Tank Engine No. 1503. The demand for a powerful locomotive for heavy banking and coal shunting resulted in an order for five 0-8-2 engines being placed on the 28th November 1907. They were completed in March/April 1908. The engines had the largest boilers then built at Horwich with the driving and third pair of wheels flangeless to facilitate rounding curves. The smokebox doors had a wheel instead of a lever fitted. The engines were finally withdrawn in June 1929.

2-6-0 'Crab' No. 13124. At the time of George Hughes's resignation as Chief Mechanical Engineer at Horwich in July 1925, he was involved in the design of a 2-6-0 engine. His chief draughtsman, G. M. Gass, continued the project in liaison with Sir Henry Fowler at Derby. The latter had his say in the design, despite advice, and the result was the construction of 30 engines, similar to the one shown in the accompanying photograph, between April 1926 and November 1927. The Lentz Poppet Valve Gear was incorporated in the design.

0-4-0 Saddle Tank Shunting Engine No. 2. Known as a 'pug' these engines were used principally around the docks at Fleetwood and Liverpool and in goods yards for shunting. All 'pugs' were either built or fitted with wooden dumb buffers. No. 2, shown in the photograph, entered service on 27 April 1910 and was withdrawn on 2nd July 1931.

0-4-0 Saddle Tank Shunting Engine No. 310. This engine built in December 1891 remained in service until September 1962.

Stanier 8F No. 48756 in Horwich Works following its refurbishment in May 1964. The works manager H. E. Kemp, Esq., can be seen standing at the microphone addressing the assembly with the Chairman of Horwich U.D.C., wearing his chain of office, to the right.

Ceremony for the last engine to be repaired at Horwich, leaving the works on the 6th May 1964.

Engine Nos. 48756 and 44308 in Horwich Locomotive Works grounds. May 1964.

The last days of steam at the works..

HORWICH RAILWAY MECHANICS' INSTITUTE

Opening programme for the Horwich Railway Mechanics' Institute.

John Audley Frederick Aspinall, who was appointed as Chief Mechanical Engineer at Horwich Locomotive Works in July 1886, wrote to the Lancashire and Yorkshire Railway Board on the 22nd November 1886 recommending the urgent introduction of a premium apprentice scheme the monies from which would fund the cost of providing a mechanics' institute. The recommendations were accepted and the institute was designed by Henry Shelmadine the architect for the L & Y Railway Co., in 1887. The Mechanics' Institute, built by Thomas Riley & Co., at a cost of £3,140, was officially opened on the 15th December 1888. Engineering Sciences were taught and up to 90 students a week were accommodated who were charged nominal fees provided that they attended at least 21 classes in each subject, otherwise the fees were doubled. Such was the success of the scheme that the institute was enlarged by the addition of two wings to the original building. A reading room, smoke room, library and a large hall capable of seating 900 persons were added along with metallurgical and other technical class rooms. A grant of £5,000 was voted by the shareholders of the L & Y Railway Co. One of the extension wings was named the Samuel Fielden Wing and it was officially opened on the 27th July 1893 along with the other extensions. The winter of 1893 saw 790 students in attendance being taught twenty distinct subjects by 16 certificated teachers. Samuel Fielden's widow donated a further sum of money to finance the provision of a gymnasium at the institute which was subsequently opened on the 26th October 1895, by John A. F. Aspinall. Following the opening ceremony those assembled were treated to a gymnastic display staged by members of the Manchester YMCA Gymnasium.

Horwich Railway Mechanics' Institute. c.1890. This photograph shows the original building with a roof cupola. Two wings were added in the 1890's - one at each end of the institute.

Horwich Railway Mechanics' Institute, Chorley New Road, Horwich. c.1902. The original institute runs parallel with Chorley New Road where the tram tracks can be seen. Two wings were subsequently added which ran at right angles to the original building. The wing on the left is the 'Samuel Fielden Wing'. A stone tablet between the upper storeys on the Chorley New Road side commemorates the gift of this wing by Mrs. Fielden in memory of her husband who for many years was a Director of the Lancashire and Yorkshire Railway Company. Monies were also provided for the second wing by Mrs. Fielden along with a gymnasium for use by the students which was formally opened on the 26th October 1895 by J. A. F. Aspinall. The monetary balance was provided by the L & YR. Co. shareholders - a total of £5,000, i.e £2,500 for each wing.

Opening programme for the extensions

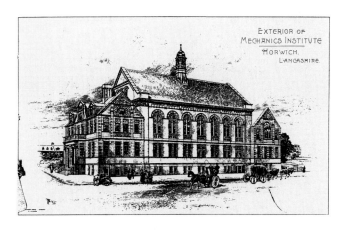

EXTERIOR OF
MECHANICS INSTITUTE
HORWICH,
LANCASHIRE.

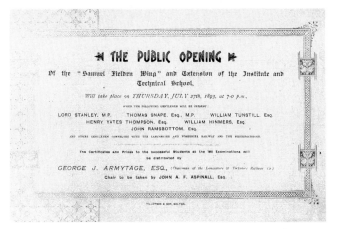

INTERIOR OF THE ART ROOM.

MECHANICS INSTITUTE HORWICH, LANCASHIRE.

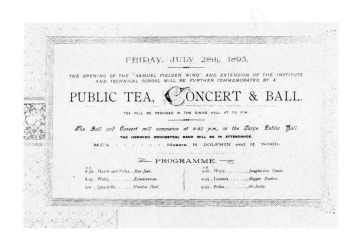

INTERIOR OF THE LARGE HALL.

MECHANICS INSTITUTE HORWICH, LANCASHIRE.

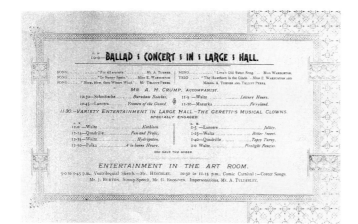

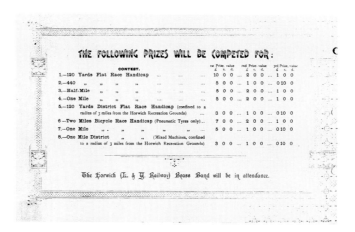

Chorley New Road, Horwich. c.1910. The first property on the left is Quinks Grocery Stores, 294 Chorley New Road. The Railway Mechanics' Institute is on the right.

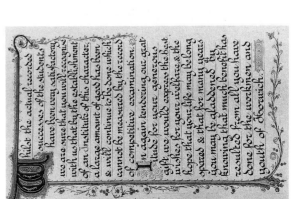

At the opening ceremony for the Samuel Fielden Wing an illuminated book was presented to Mrs Fielden by the L & Y Railway Company Directors. Extracts from the book are included above.

Chemical and Mechanical Laboratories.

During 1901, Chemical and Mechanical Laboratories were provided at the Fox Street end of the Institute funded by the further generosity of Mrs Fielden, in remembrance of her husband Samuel Fielden.

Chemistry Laboratory at the Mechanics' Institute. c.1902.

Mechanical Science Laboratory. c.1902.

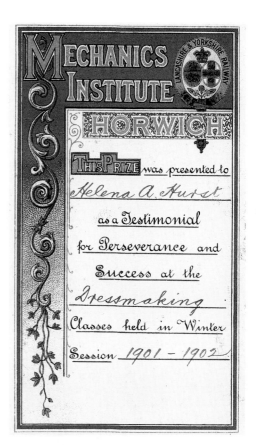

John McLean, Librarian at the Horwich Mechanics' Institute from 1888 - 1929. He was born in Scotland moving to Horwich to take up a position with the L & Y Railway Company as librarian at the Mechanics' Institute when it opened. During his time at Horwich he lived in Fox Street and Crown Lane but moved into 71 Victoria Road, Horwich during 1904. He remained there until his death in the late 1940's.

Bookplate from a prize presented to Helena A. Hurst in the Winter Session, 1901 - 1902 for Dressmaking.

Horwich Railway Mechanics' Institute Gymnasium. c.1920. John McLean, who was the librarian at the institute from 1888 until 1929, is pictured with Inspector Ryder and the officers of Horwich Section of the Lancashire Constabulary.

Railway Mechanics' Institute.

CHORLEY NEW ROAD, HORWICH

Election of Six Committee Men to serve from January, 1900, to January, 1901.

MEMBERS NOMINATED.			
Surname.	Christian Name.	Occupation.	VOTE.
CHAMPION	CHARLES F.	Foreman	
DUDDING	JAMES	Foreman	
FINNEY	HENRY	Fitter	
PEERS	TELLITT	Foreman	
ROBERTS	JOSEPH H.	Millwright	
SLADE	FARNHAM	Foreman	
THORNHAM	FRANCIS	Foreman	

Every Member over eighteen years of age has **SIX** Votes. A Member can vote for Six or a less number of Candidates, but no Candidate can receive more than **ONE** vote from each Member.

Members must place a **X** opposite the names of the Candidates for whom they wish to vote.

The Voting Paper of any Member who has marked crosses against the names of more than Six Candidates will be cancelled.

The Voting Papers must be placed in the Ballot Box, which for that purpose will be kept in the Library, at any time from Monday, January 8th, at 12.30 p.m., to Monday, January 15th, 1900, at 7.30 p.m., when the General Meeting will be held.

Ballot paper for the election of six committee members to serve in 1900.

Cast of Horwich Operatic Society's production of the Mikado in 1922. Among the players are Sydney Hanson, Marjorie Davies and Frances Walton.

Technical Drawing Classes for 1911 and 1912 photographed in the Mechanics' Institute Gymnasium. Samuel Drinkwater who taught the subject appears on the extreme left in both photographs - seated in the one taken in 1912.

Above: Henry Fowler with his sister. c.1889. Henry Fowler was born at Evesham, Worcestershire, on the 29th July 1870. From 1887 until 1891 he was apprenticed under Aspinall at Horwich Works where in 1891 he gained the first Whitworth Exhibition to be awarded to a member of the Horwich Mechanics' Institute. He later became a teacher at the Institute leaving in 1900 to take up a post with the Midland Railway at Derby.

Letter written by John McLean for donations to a leaving present for Henry Fowler. 1900.

Right: Henry Fowler maintained his friendship with John McLean after leaving Horwich.

Above: James Tatlow who was secretary to the Mechanics' Institute from the time it opened. Photo c.1890.

Ernest Roberts who succeeded John McLean as librarian of the Mechanics' Institute in 1929.

Copy of a letter from James T. Tatlow to John McLean.

ROYAL HOTEL,
DERBY.

April 2ⁿᵈ 1901

My dear MacLean

In August or September of last year (1900) the drivers and firemen – with other branches of the service – of the Great Eastern R760, made an application to the Directors of that Co – for an increase of wages and reduction of working hours &c –

The matter was fully discussed in the newspapers at the time and I want you to find the copies of the "Times" containing

Ⓐ The terms of application for increased wages reduced hours by the Drivers & firemen and

Ⓑ The final decision of the

Gt Eastern Directors.

Please send them to Ravenstone Common (Wednesday) that I may see them on my return at 9.25 pm tomorrow night.

Yours faithfully

J.T.Tatlow

125

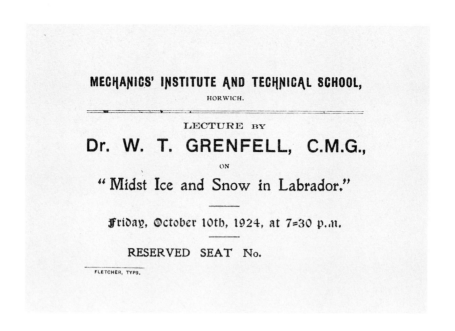

MECHANICS' INSTITUTE AND TECHNICAL SCHOOL,

HORWICH.

LECTURE BY

Dr. W. T. GRENFELL, C.M.G.,

ON

" Midst Ice and Snow in Labrador."

Friday, October 10th, 1924, at 7=30 p.m.

RESERVED SEAT No.

FLETCHER, TYPS.

Ticket for a lecture at the Mechanics' Institute on the 10th October 1924.

CHORLEY NEW ROAD, HORWICH.

Horwich Mechanics' Institute. c.1920.

THE LANCASHIRE AND YORKSHIRE ARMS.

The L & Y Railway Co. land agent and architect, Henry Shelmadine, who was responsible for the design of the Mechanics' Institute on Chorley New Road, also designed the L & Y. Arms which stood at the corner of Chorley New Road and Gooch Street. Neill & Sons submitted a successful tender of £1,627 for building the property. It was originally intended that the premises should be licensed for the sale of intoxicants, but the application for a Justices' Licence was refused by the Bolton licensing Committee on the grounds that there was no need for a further licensed outlet in the area already well serviced by retail outlets for intoxicants. The cafe, as it became known, had a resident manager and catered for a variety of social functions as well as providing accommodation. Many of the properties in Horwich did not possess a bath at this time, other than perhaps a zinc tub, and it was common for local people to use the bathing facilities at the L & Y. Arms for which there was a modest charge.

L & Y Cafe, Chorley New Road, Horwich. c.1902.

Railway cafe sentenced

Horwich Railway Cafe—sentenced to demolition.

OLD HORWICH BUILDING HIT BY DRY ROT

THE Railway Cafe—a familiar meeting spot for Horwich people since before the turn of the century—is shortly to fall under the hammer.

Dry rot has attacked the three-storey building, and the front portion will have to be demolished. A British Rail spokesman said: "This part of the building has been badly damaged by the fungus and is considered unsafe. It will be pulled down before Christmas."

Preparatory work for the demolition was in progress this week, including the removal of inscribed windows, which are to be kept at the York Railway Museum.

Many people will probably feel a tinge of sadness at the disappearance of the cafe frontage on Chorley New Road. It is a building which had strong links with the railway history of the town.

It is thought to have been built around 1880, and was originally intended as a public house. In fact the inscription "L and Y Arms" can still be seen in the frosted glass of the building's windows.

But an objection by the Bolton Licensing Authority that drinkers were well catered for by nearby pubs was upheld. However, the cafe became well known as a meeting place for many local organisations and for many years it was the only place where many Horwichites could get a proper bath.

NO BATHS

Mr James Hester, of Fox Street, Horwich, remembers visiting it as a young man.

"In those days many houses in Horwich had no baths, except for the zinc ones.

One of the Railway Cafe windows showing the "L & Y Arms" inscription.

When you got too old to use that you went to the railway cafe," he recalled. "This went on until about 1930."

Mr Hester also pointed out that several local organisations had their origins at the railway cafe. For instance the Horwich works committee and the railway veterans held their first meetings there.

"I am sure that quite a chunk of Horwich's history was shaped inside that building," he added.

● A tender — of £1,627 for the construction of the dining hall 'L and Y Arms' was let in 1887.

THE L. & Y. ARMS

CAFÉ AND RESTAURANT

(Adjoining the Railway Works),

Chorley New Road, Horwich,

Is replete with every convenience for Large or Small Parties.

A capital Bill of Fare, consisting of SOUPS, ENTREES, JOINTS, SWEETS, &c., is provided every Day, from 12 to 2. **Prices very moderate.**

BREAD AND CONFECTIONERY MADE AND BAKED ON THE PREMISES.

BILLIARDS, CHESS, DRAUGHTS, &c.

Beds, Private Sitting-Room, Lavatories and Baths.

SPECIAL ARRANGEMENTS for Schools, Pic-nic and Private Parties, may be made on application to the

Resident Manager - GEORGE J. CLUEARD.

The above Establishment is a Branch of The Central Tea and Coffee Houses Company, Limited, Manchester.

FRANK SHORT, General Manager.

P.S.—Special attention is paid to the Beds.

Advertisement for the L & Y Arms from the Horwich Post Office Directory for 1890.

Newspaper report from the Horwich and Westhoughton Journal dated 3/11/1972 concerning the demolition of the L & Y Cafe.

THE 'CAT' OFF-LICENCE

Off-licence, Watts Street / Chorley New Road, Horwich. c.1910. Matthew Cuthrie was the licensee of the premises at the time of this photograph. The off-licence was known locally as the 'Cat' and the group of men outside were employees at Horwich Locomotive Works. They seem to be dressed for an outing. The premises were well patronised by the employees at the works because they could not obtain intoxicating drink at either the L & Y Arms or the works refreshment room. Working in close proximity to molten metal, particularly during the summer months, meant that it was only natural for workmen to 'slake' their thirst.

Workers pose for a photograph c. 1920. A beer bottle is between the two men.

Close up of group outside the 'Cat'. The man seated front right is John Greenhalgh who was a steel moulder on Horwich Locomotive Works. He died in May 1919.

Opposite top: Horwich Locomotive Works Fire Train and Van. c.1902.

Opposite bottom: Horwich Locomotive Works Fire Brigade with their moveable 'Merryweather' Fire Engine. c.1902.

THE LANCASHIRE AND YORKSHIRE RAILWAY FIRE BRIGADE.

The Lancashire and Yorkshire Railway Company maintained a works fire brigade at Horwich Locomotive Works comprised of employees. There was a completely fitted fire train with an engine in steam nearby ready to proceed to any fire alarm. The firemen were summoned by a coded use of the Works buzzer and as many were housed in streets close to the works there was little delay in obtaining a full turnout of the fire crew. A moveable pump and equipment were also provided for attending fires in the town.

The Lancashire County Council eventually took over the responsibilty for the provision of fire cover and a fire station was built near the work's entrance in 1939. At the time of writing, this fire station has been demolished and is to be replaced with an entirely new building.

Horwich L & Y Railway Co.
Firemen training at the works.
c.1915.

This training session took place on the recreation ground. The bandstand can be seen to the left with Ramsbottom Road in the background. c.1915.

The L & Y Railway Co. Fire Brigade are pictured attending a fire in Fox Street. The 'Samuel Fielden Wing' of the Mechanics' Institute is to the left with the 'L & Y' Cafe on the right. c.1915.

RECREATION GROUND

On the 23rd April 1892 a large recreation ground comprising two bowling greens, tennis courts, a cricket ground and children's playground was opened on the north side of Chorley New Road almost opposite the Work's entrance. Funding for the recreation ground was provided by two Lancashire and Yorkshire Railway Company Directors - William Hinmers and Henry Yates Thompson. The latter also provided a bandstand in the recreation ground which was built in June 1907.

Left: Entrance to the L & Y Railway Recreation Ground, Ramsbottom Road, Horwich c.1915. The cricket field is in the foreground with the tennis court visible to the right.

Below: Pavilion in L & Y Railway Recreation Ground, Horwich. c.1900. The wooden structure was eventually demolished in 1980 and replaced with a brick building.

Above: L & Y. R. Loco' Prize Band, Horwich. c.1912.

Below: View of the bandstand with Ramsbottom Road in the background. c.1912.

BANDSTAND AND RECREATION GROUND, HORWICH

Plaque from the bandstand in the L & Y Railway Recreation Ground, Horwich. 1907.

Tennis Courts L & Y Railway Recreation Ground, Horwich. c.1905. The tennis courts on the recreation ground were opened for play in May 1905.

View of one of the bowling greens with a children's play area behind. c.1900. The tower of Horwich Parish Church is seen in the background.

Horwich Locomotive Work's Hockey Team. 1920.

The cricket field and pavilion. c.1920.

Horwich Railway Mechanics' Institute (RMI) Band

The Lancashire & Yorkshire Railway Works at Horwich had its own band which was not particularly successful and in 1912 George Hughes, CME, proposed a reformation to improve standards. Auditions were held and only one member of the existing L & YR Company Band was successful, the remaining band members being selected from several other established bands. On its formation the new band was renamed the Horwich RMI Band.

In 1915 the Horwich RMI Band was beaten into second place in the September Brass Band Championships held at Belle Vue, Manchester, by Foden's Motor Works Band. A short time after the championships several members of the Foden's Band were sacked following a strike and joined the Horwich RMI Band in retaliation. The upshot was that in the 1916 Belle Vue contest Foden's Motor Works Band came second to the Horwich RMI Band.

The crowning glory for the Horwich RMI Band came on the 23rd September 1922 when they won the prestigious Crystal Palace Trophy, effectively making them champions of Great Britain and the Colonies.

Mr. G. HINKINSON,
Solo Trombone.

Mr. J. BROOKES,
Solo Soprano Cornet.

Mr. ARTHUR RILEY,
Secretary.

Mr. H. SUTCLIFFE,
Conductor.

Mr. A. HAZLEHURST,
Solo Cornet.

Mr. R. SMITH,
Solo Euphonium.

Members of the Horwich RMI Band.

HORWICH
RAILWAY MECHANICS'
INSTITUTE
BRASS BAND.
—o—
RULES.

1. Membership of the Band shall be restricted to members of the Institute who are employees of the Lancashire and Yorkshire Railway Company.

2. The subscription shall be one penny per week, and members may give signed authority for this to be deducted from their wages.

3. The Annual Meeting shall be held in December of each year, when there shall be elected for the ensuing twelve months a President, Vice-Presidents, Auditors, Secretary, Treasurer, and Committee—three members of which shall be subscribers' representatives.

BENEFITS
OF MEMBERSHIP.
❖

1. The Band to give three Concerts a year in the Railway Mechanics' Institute, and members of the Band to be entitled to two free reserved seats (allocated by ballot) for each Concert.

2. A Social and Dance to be held annually, for which members will receive two free tickets.

3. Members to have the exclusive right to be present at rehearsals conducted by the professional tutor, and each to be entitled to bring one friend.

4. During the summer concerts in the Recreation Ground, certain seats to be reserved for members.

NAME OF MEMBER :

Copy of the Rules for members of
Horwich RMI Band.

Horwich RMI Band with the Crystal Palace Trophy won on the 23rd September 1922.

Recreational facilities

Before the Railway Mechanics' Institute opened on the 15th December 1888; Horwich Public Hall, situated on Lee Lane, was the centre for much of the social and recreational activity of the town. The building of the Public Hall was financed by Peter Martin of The Street, Rivington, and he officially opened it for public use on the 2nd April 1879.

Excellent facilities existed at the Mechanics' Institute for both study and recreation and this combination eventually led to a decline in popularity of the Public Hall with the Institute becoming the new leisure centre.

In the 1890's when 5,000 men and boys were employed at the Locomotive Works, no fewer than 2,224 were regularly involved in either the study classes or the sporting and recreational pursuits at the Institute.

In addition to the more conventional games including football, cricket, hockey, tennis and bowls; a rifle club was founded in April 1910 and the Horwich RMI Operatic Society first performed in 1913. There was also a keen interest in photography and trips were frequently arranged to beauty spots up and down the country. Concessionary travel arrangements available to railway employees brought a wide range of destinations within any financial constraints.

A number of photographs are included to illustrate some of the activities referred to although each club and society is deserving of special mention.

Members of the Horwich RMI Camera Club. 1908.

Horwich RMI Camera Club on assignment in Dean Wood, Rivington. 1910.

John McLean, Secretary of the Mechanics' Institute on the rifle range at Horwich Locomotive Works. c.1910.

Horwich Locomotive Works Boiler Makers' picnic to the Dukeries, Nottingham, on the 16th April 1894.

Horwich Drawing Office picnic. 1910.

PROGRAMME.

1. Ron Wotherspoon
   B.B.C. Vibraphone and Xylophonist
   presents "Sticks in Tempo."

2. Horwich Senior Girls' School Choir
   by kind permission of Miss D. H. Green, B.A.
   Conductor — Miss M. Calderwood.
   Accompanist — Madam Harrison.
   (a) The Dance ... two part *Edward Elgar*
   (b) Fly, Singing Bird, Fly three part *Edward Elgar*
   (c) Lift Thine Eyes three part *From Elijah Mendelssohn*
   (d) Shepherds' Dance two part *From Henry VIII Ed. German*

3. Speciality Dancing by Jean Roberts
   (a) Hungarian Dance
   (b) Tarantelle Dance

4. Pianoforte Solo by Geoffrey Bain
   Andante and Rondo Capricciosi
   by Felix Mendelssohn—Bartholdy. Op. 14.

5. NORMAN EVANS
   Lancashire's Ambassador of Mirth.
   Stage and Radio Star
   ROYAL COMMAND 1937.

6. Selection by S.S. Peter and Paul's Girls' School
   By kind permission of Mother Hyacinth.

7. Bill Pearce
   Piano—Accordian.

8. NAUGHTON, AND GOLD
   Stars of Crazy Gang — London Palladium.

9. Mavis and Doreen
   Horwich Radio and Stage Duettists.
   Accompanist—Margaret C. Roskelly, A.R.M.C.M.
   (a) I heard a Voice in the Tranquil Night—*Glover*
   (b) The Old Sweet Song—*Caprice Viennois Kreisler*
   (c) Lo! Here the Gentle Lark—*Sir Henry Bishop*

Select ✦ Concert

in the

Railway Mechanics' Institute

on

Sunday, October 3rd, 1943,

at 6-40 p.m. prompt.

by

ALL STAR ARTISTS.

ARRANGED AND PRESENTED BY
NORMAN HOLDEN.

TOTAL PROCEEDS TO LOCAL AND POLICE CHARITIES.

FLETCHER, HORWICH.

10. THE TWO PAIGES
    Fashions in Dancing.

11. Martin Milner and His Violin
    (a) Andante-Presto *by Tartini*
    (b) Rondino *by Kreisler*
    (c) Scherzo-Tarantelle *by Wieniawski*

12. BILLY SCOTT COOMBER AND JEANETTE HALEY
    with Bill Pearce at the Piano.

13. NORMAN EVANS

14. HAROLD RAMSEY & CHERRIE COOPER
    Featuring THEATRE ORGAN.

    Accompanist ... ... Mrs. J. HILL
    Stage Manager ... Mr. S. HANSON.

    SHOW CONCLUDES 9-55 P.M.

    Trams available after Show to Bolton and Horwich.
    Air Raid Shelters — Fox Street and Brunel Street.
    Air Raid Warning will be announced from stage.

    ### APRECIATION.

    To all who have assisted me in the organising of this Concert,
    especially the Artists who have given their services entirely free,
    Inspector R. A. McGeoch, E. Roberts, F. Roberts, W. Haydock,
    S. Hanson, H. Lomax, W. Edwards, F. Abbott, I sincerely thank
    you. The proceeds totaling £100 will be allocated as follows:—
    Bolton Royal Infirmary £35
    Northern Police Convalescent Home ... £35
    Horwich Sick Nursing Association £15
    Horwich Tuberculosis After Care Committee £15
    Yours truly,
    NORMAN HOLDEN.

Programme for a concert at the Railway Mechanics' Institute on the 3rd October 1943.

142

Horwich Operatic Society. 1960. The Operatic Society, originally formed in 1913, was re-formed in 1954 following the Second World War. The photograph was taken in the large hall at the Institute.

The Railway Mechanics' Institute. c.1960.

L & Y RAILWAY COTTAGE HOSPITAL

Henry Yates Thompson whose gifts to the town of Horwich included the locomotive work's recreation ground and a bandstand, also provided monies which enabled the construction of the Cottage Hospital during 1894. The hospital was for the treatment of accidents that occurred in the works although a number of local firms were permitted to use the facilities of the hospital for accidents occurring on their own premises.

During the 1914 - 1918 World War, the L & Y Railway Cottage Hospital was used for wounded servicemen to convalesce.

The provision of hospitals by the County Council phased out the need for the Cottage Hospital which was eventually sold. It is presently used by a private company.

L & Y Cottage Hospital, Brunel Street, Horwich. c.1900.

By contributing to the hospital fund members were accorded special treatment and convalescent privileges.

L. M. & S. RLY.
HOSPITAL FUND.
District No. 56

MEMBERSHIP CARD.

This is to certify that 3568

W. S. Brown

is a contributor to the above Fund.

Wm. Haslam.

Branch Secretary.

R. E. LYON,
Secretary,
Crewe Station.

This card must not be used for obtaining treatment at Hospitals, but produced when applying for RECOMMENDS OR GRANTS.

Matron Jubb seated at her desk in the L & Y Cottage Hospital, Horwich. c.1910.

HORWICH LOCOMOTIVE WORK'S MANAGEMENT STRUCTURE.

John Audley Frederick Aspinall was the first appointment at Horwich Locomotive Works to carry the title of Chief Mechanical Engineer. His second in command was the Works Manager - Henry Albert Hoy.

A list of the men in charge at Horwich follows, together with a series of photographs, and a miscellany of information relating to a cross selection of the overall activities of the management team members throughout the years.

Chief Mechanical Engineer.   Works Manager.

J. A. F. Aspinall	1886 - 1889	H. A. Hoy	1887 - 1889
H. A. Hoy	1889 - 1904	George Hughes	1889 - 1904
George Hughes	1904 - 1925	Oliver Winder	1904 - 1909
		John Peachey Crouch	1909 - 1910
		H. Eoghan O'Brien	1910 - 1924

During the First World War, H. E. O'Brien was called up for active service and George Nuttall Shawcross was appointed as Acting Works Manager until O'Brien returned in 1918. O'Brien's title on his return was Works Manager and Electrical Engineer. Shawcross became Mechanical Engineer and Works Manager on O'Brien's resignation in 1924 and remained in this capacity until 1936.

Following the retirement of George Hughes in 1925 the Chief Mechanical Engineer was no longer based at Horwich which left the Works Manager / Superintendent in charge - whose title varied as indicated below.

D. Williamson	Works Superintendent	1936 - 1951
S. A. S. Smith	Works Manager	1952 - 1956
E. R. Brown	Works Manager	1956 - 1959
R. C. S. Low	Works Manager	1959 - 1962
A. T. Garnett	Works Manager	1962 - 1963
Major H. E. Kemp	Works Manager	1963 - 1968
E. T. Butcher	Works Manager	1968 - 1971
G. F. S. Staley	Works Manager	1971 - 1976
G. M. James	Works Manager	1976 - 1978
C. P. J. Sheppard	Works Manager	1978 - 1983

Sir John A. F. Aspinall.

H. A. Hoy, Esq.

George Hughes.

George Nuttall Shawcross.

D. Williamson.

S. A. S. Smith.

E. R. Brown.

R. C. S. Low.

A. T. Garnett.

Major H. E. Kemp.

E. T. Butcher.

G. F. S. Staley.

G. M. James.

C. P. J. Sheppard 1978 - 1983

Edward Mellor Gass, born in 1861 was appointed as leading draughtsman at Horwich Locomotive Works in 1888. He was largely responsible for the detailed design work on the locomotives of Aspinall, Hoy and Hughes. He retired from Horwich in 1926.

Presentation to E. R. Brown on his leaving Horwich Locomotive Works in 1959. The photograph was taken in the conference room at the works.

R. C. S. Low, Works Manager, conducting presentation ceremonies at the works.

Works personnel on the lawn outside the main entrance to Horwich Locomotive Works, with the Works Manager A. T. Garnett.

A. T. Garnett, Works Manager, conducts a presentation to William Bowen to mark his retirement.

Works personnel photographed with A. T. Garnett. Hawkshaw Street can be seen in the background.

H. E. Kemp, Works Manager, makes a presentation in the conference room at the works.

Staff photograph taken on the lawn near the Work's entrance with the fire brigade tower visible to the right. The Work's Manager, R. C. S. Low is in the centre of the picture.

HORWICH LOCOMOTIVE WORKS DURING THE FIRST WORLD WAR. 1914 - 1918.

Whilst the political situation in Europe worsened following the assassination of Archduke Francis Ferdinand, heir to the Hapsburg thrones, at Sarajevo on the 28th June 1914; both Sir George Armytage and John A. F. Aspinall - the Chairman and General Manager respectively, of the L & Y Railway Company - took their annual summer holiday in the German Spa of Bad Homburg during July 1914. Austria - Hungary declared war against Serbia on the 28th July 1914 and Germany declared war against Russia and France on the 1st and 3rd August, respectively, with Great Britain declaring war against Germany on the 4th August 1914. Sir George Armytage managed to leave Germany in the nick of time but John A. F. Aspinall was unable to secure a passage out mainly because civilian railway travel in Germany was suspended on the 1st August 1914. On the 17th August 1914 Aspinall and his party subsequently managed to get a train to Cologne where they intended to board a Rhine steamer for Rotterdam but they were stopped and Aspinall, together with another male travelling in his party, were interned in a military prison. Frantic efforts were made to secure the release of Aspinall and his friend with the fortunate result that they were eventually allowed to leave Germany arriving in Folkestone on the 24th September 1914.

Great Britain's 'call to arms' resulted in a flood of volunteers for active service, including many railwaymen. This situation left the various railway company managements in somewhat of a dilemma because the railroads were needed to play an important role if victory was to be secured and proper operations were prejudiced by so many men leaving their jobs to enlist in the armed forces. On the other hand, any check placed on railway employees to join the armed forces could be interpreted as unpatriotic. In the event a compromise was reached and war recruitment agencies only signed up men in railway employ provided that they could be spared from their civilian duties.

Prior to the 1914 - 1918 World War there were 120 separate railway companies in Great Britain. The railways were essentially a male domain employing only 13,046 women in 1913, 8,482 on domestic duties and 4,564 on clerical work related to the railways proper. With so many railwaymen enlisting for the armed forces following the outbreak of war it fell to the women to fill the serious labour deficiency created. The Railway Executive formed a sub-committee to assess the feasibility of employing women in grades formerly held by men. Heavy manual duties such as engine driving and firing were not considered appropriate. One condition insisted upon by the National Union of Railwaymen to protect members' jobs on their eventual return, was that women should

only be employed on a temporary basis. This meant that there was no proper career structure for women and no chance of advancement. It led to many women leaving after a very short period to work in the munitions factories. Throughout the period of hostilities women proved their worth in many skilled situations, so much so that in 1920 after the war had ended some 20,000 women were still employed in grades where their skills had become appreciated.

Horwich Locomotive Works was first involved in war production during the Autumn of 1914 when the Railway Executive agreed to the use of railway workshops to aid the war effort provided that it did not materially affect any company's ability to fulfil its primary role of the repair and replacement of railway equipment. The main responsibilities at Horwich were the production of fuses and shells and the renovation of cartridge cases but the works were also involved in specific projects such as the development of an electro-magnetic roller intended for picking up ferrous scrap metal from battlefields.

In addition to his duties in overall control of war production of munitions, etc., John A. F. Aspinall was instrumental in extending the railway electrification scheme first introduced on the Liverpool - Southport - Crossens line on the 13th May 1904. H. Eoghan O'Brien, who had been in charge of the Liverpool - Southport - Crossens electrification scheme moved to Newton Heath in 1909 and in the following year was appointed as Assistant Chief Mechanical Engineer at Horwich Locomotive Works under George Hughes.

Dick, Kerr and Company, of Preston, carried out much of the work associated with the electrification scheme and subsequently kept in close contact with Aspinall concerning developments. In 1913 the company advised Aspinall when a Brazilian railway enquired regarding the construction of locomotives operating at 3,500 volts DC. Aspinall arranged for a section of steeply graded track between Bury and Holcombe Brook to be used in the project, provided that no expense fell on the L & Y Railway Company. Despite gradients of 1 in 50 and 1 in 40 the new electrically powered locomotives proved successful. Aspinall adopted the idea and obtained authorisation to electrify a stretch of line between Manchester and Bury. Instead of using the 3,500 volt system he opted for 1,200 volts DC, with third rail pick up and fourth rail return. The project was scheduled for completion in 1915 but the outbreak of hostilities slowed up the electrification scheme, although work did continue under the direction of George Hughes and Douglas Campbell Rattray the chief civil engineer.

H. E. O'Brien, the acknowledged electrical expert on the L & Y Railway, was called up for military service to command the 111th Company, Railway Troops, Royal Engineers. Although O'Brien was released from his command in 1915 he did not return to Horwich but took over an important post in the Ministry of Munitions where he remained throughout the remainder of the war.

The Manchester to Bury electrification scheme scheduled for completion in 1915 was eventually brought into service in February 1916. Therefore in the first eighteen months of the war, Horwich Locomotive Works was engaged in the electrification scheme in addition to war work. Although no new passenger engines were built at Horwich during the war years, four Aspinall 0-6-0 goods engines were constructed from available spare parts in 1917, 24 large-boilered superheated 0-8-0s, and 20 non-superheated 0-8-0s also left the works between August 1914 and December 1918. This relatively small amount of locomotive production gives some indication of the extent to which Horwich Locomotive Works was involved in the war effort. In comparison, the railway works at Crewe belonging to the London and North Western Railway were able to construct some 200 new engines during the war years, one of which, No. 2395, built in 1916, was named J. A. F. Aspinall. It was rather unusual that when Aspinall was created a Knight Bachelor in the 1917 King's Birthday Honours List the engine bearing his name was not subsequently changed to Sir J. A. F. Aspinall.

On the 8th June 1915, following setbacks in the battle against Germany, a Ministry of Munitions was formed which immediately ordered the machining of 2,250 shells per week. These munitions were principally provided by seven railway companies including the Lancashire and Yorkshire Railway Company. There is no doubt that the operations at Horwich during the First World War played an important part in the eventual victory.

The illustrations included below show local people, principally women, involved in war work at Horwich Locomotive Works during the 1914 - 1918 conflict and the cenotaph erected near the works entrance to honour those workers who made the supreme sacrifice.

Motor Shop - L & Y Railway Company. 1914 - 1918

Projectiles - World War ammunition. 1914 - 1918

Women at work in the Machine Shop at Horwich - 1914 - 1918

Woman working with a band-saw at
Horwich Works. 1914 - 1918

Shell Shop (formerly The Forge) c.1917. -
Refurbishing shell cases.

Above: World War I - Horwich Works. c.1917.

Below: Production of shell cases at Horwich Works. c.1917. This building was later to be named the "Bullet Shop".

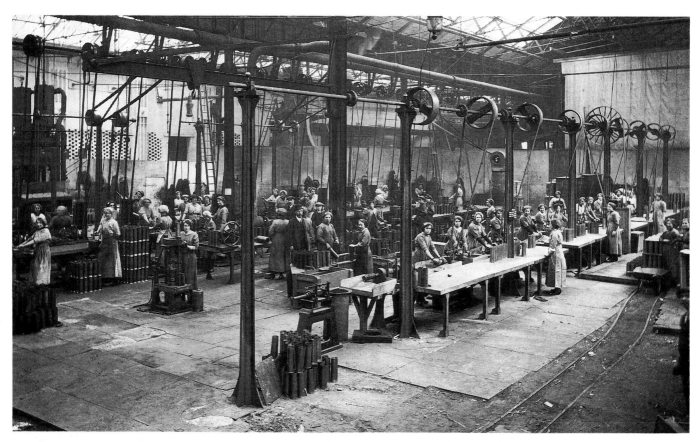

Above: Women refurbishing shell cases in the Shell Shop (Forge). c.1917.

Below: Joiners' Shop. c.1917

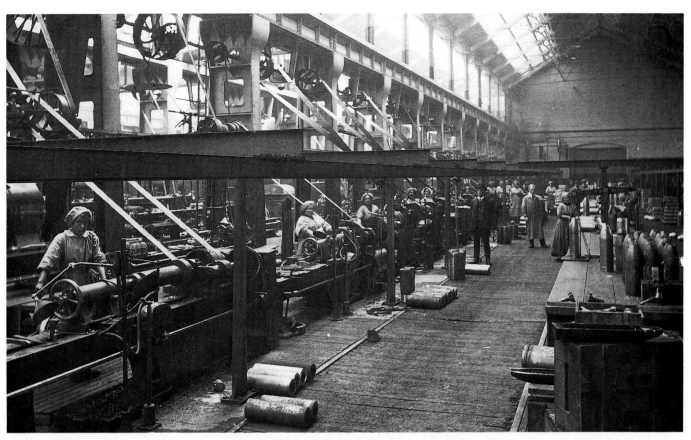

Above: Shell manufacture in the erecting shop.

Below: Shell Shop (Forge) L & Y Railway Company Works, Horwich. 1914 - 1918

Fitting Shop L & Y Railway Company Works, Horwich. 1914 - 1918

L & Y Railway Company Motor Shop, Horwich. 1918. Thomas Clayton the Motor Shop Foreman is seated front centre.

War work in the Shell Shop. 1914 - 1918.

The wooden annexe building in which the women are working was situated in the works yard. 1914 - 1918.

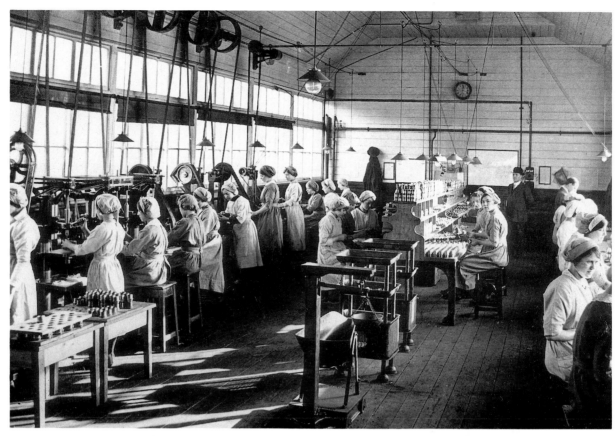

Another view of the inside of the wooden annexe. 1914 - 1918.

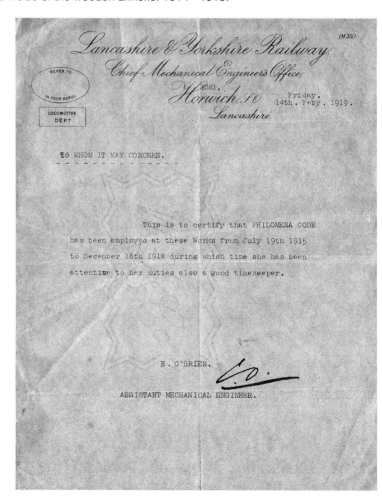

Work reference for Miss Philomena Code signed by the Assistant Mechanical Engineer Mr. Eoghan O'Brien. 1919.

This electro-magnetic roller was developed at Horwich Locomotive Works during the First World War and was intended for picking up ferrous scrap metal on battlefields..

Railway engines in Horwich Locomotive Works awaiting transhipment to France for use during the 1914-1918 War.

Following the end of the war a celebration of Victory was held at the Railway Mechanics' Institute on Wednesday 12th February 1919.

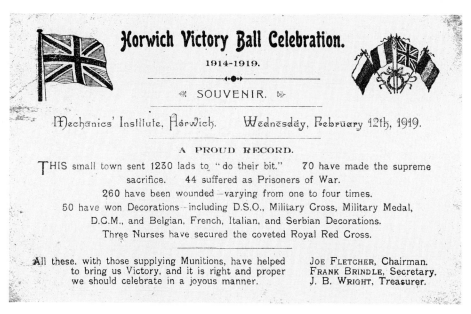

Horwich Victory Ball Celebration.
1914-1919.

SOUVENIR.

Mechanics' Institute, Horwich.   Wednesday, February 12th, 1919.

A PROUD RECORD.

THIS small town sent 1230 lads to "do their bit."   70 have made the supreme sacrifice.   44 suffered as Prisoners of War.
260 have been wounded—varying from one to four times.
50 have won Decorations—including D.S.O., Military Cross, Military Medal, D.C.M., and Belgian, French, Italian, and Serbian Decorations.
Three Nurses have secured the coveted Royal Red Cross.

All these, with those supplying Munitions, have helped to bring us Victory, and it is right and proper we should celebrate in a joyous manner.

JOE FLETCHER, Chairman.
FRANK BRINDLE, Secretary.
J. B. WRIGHT, Treasurer.

Horwich Victory Ball Celebration. 1919

Although the invitation to the victory ball refers to a contingent of 1,230 men who enlisted from Horwich, 70 of whom were killed in action; it seems that full particulars had not been collated at that time for obvious reasons. The 1914-1918 War Memorial Plaque in the Public Hall at Horwich contains the names of 219 men who were killed in action and refers to 1,500 men having enlisted from Horwich district.

The L & YR Company erected their own war memorial near to the works entrance which was unveiled by George Hughes, C M E., on 27th August 1921. The names of 120 railway employees are recorded on the L & YR Memorial. Local men who worked at Horwich Locomotive Works are honoured by having their names on both memorials.

A public Garden of Remembrance was erected near to the entrance to Lever Park in the 1950's..

Horwich Locomotive Works War Memorial.

BETWEEN THE WARS

Mergers

As early as 1871 the respective Boards of the L & YR and the L & NWR Companies had discussed a merger but a Parliamentary Committee had refused sanction at that time on the grounds that such an amalgamation was considered too monopolistic. Nevertheless, a number of agreements existed which allowed the two companies to operate certain undertakings jointly to their mutual benefit.

The Transport Act of 1921 provided for the grouping of all British railways into four large main line companies with effect from January 1923. Despite this, a decision was taken to amalgamate the operations of the L & YR and the L & NWR on a date prior to that laid down by statute. In preparation for the merger, Arthur Watson, who was the general manager of the L & YR Company, was also appointed as general manager of the L & NWR Company, to replace Sir Thomas Williams, during 1920, effectively becoming responsible for both concerns. In addition, shareholders of both companies had been made aware of the impending merger and by May 1921 had been advised of the means by which they could exchange L & YR Company stocks for those of the newly intended L & NWR Company.

On the 1st January 1922, the expected merger took place and the L & YR Company ceased to have a separate identity. The combined network was divided geographically into two divisions, all railway operations south of Crewe became Division A of the L & NWR while everything north of Crewe fell within Division B.

George Hughes was appointed as Chief Mechanical Engineer of the new combine mainly on the grounds of seniority. His opposite number at Crewe, Major Hewitt Pearson Montague Beames, had only been appointed as Chief Mechanical Engineer at Crewe on the 1st December 1920 and although he remained at Crewe he was subordinate to George Hughes. A number of other senior appointments, including that of Secretary of the combined company, went to L & YR men, which was the cause of much resentment amongst Crewe personnel who naturally preferred their own supervisors to be elected.

Many of the workshop practices being followed at Crewe at the time of the amalgamation were obsolete, particularly when taking into account the rapid advances in production engineering which had been brought about by pure necessity during the war. Horwich Locomotive Works employed far higher standards than were in force at Crewe and George Hughes made efforts to improve the situation at Crewe but met with much resistance from Beames. A standard workshop practice on the L & YR was to thoroughly examine a locomotive at least two months before it was to undergo a statutory repair visit to the workshop and compile a report on the major work required. The purpose of this was to provide advance information which was useful in structuring a proper programme for carrying out repairs, ensuring that appropriate workshop accommodation was available and deciding upon replacement engines during the time that locomotives were out of service. Beames claimed that this practice would cost £3,000 per year to implement at Crewe and the exercise would serve no useful purpose.

A system of interchange of visits of supervisory personnel was arranged between Horwich and Crewe Workshops which assisted in the identification of best workshop practices and ensured that there was a cross-flow of information.

If nothing else the early merger of the L & YR and the L & NWR served both to highlight deficiencies and provided a proving ground for senior management. There was however insufficient time in which to carry out any radical change and the railway operations remained virtually the same as they had been previously.

Horwich becomes part of the London Midland and Scottish Railway

Whatever difficulties existed in the 1922 merger were insignificant compared to those experienced in the railway groupings which came into effect on the 1st January 1923. Considering that the Parliamentary Committee of 1871 felt that the merger of the L & YR and the L & NWR was too monopolistic, it is odd that the much larger amalgamation was allowed without comment. The following companies pooled their operations on the appointed date to become the London Midland and Scottish Railway Company:- L & YR, L & NWR, Midland Railway, Caledonian Railway, Glasgow and South Western Railway, Highland Railway, Furness Railway and the North Staffordshire Railway.

Appointments to the board of the newly formed LMSR were to prove crucial when it came to deciding upon the policies and procedures to be followed by such a large conglomerate. The locomotive stock of the combine amounted to 10,316 locomotives of 393 different types. An immediate policy of reducing the number of types by developing a core of standard engines was introduced. The Honourable C. N. Lawrence (L & NWR) became Chairman, with Deputy Chairmen Sir Guy Granet (Midland) and E. B. Fielden (L & YR). George Hughes was appointed as Chief Mechanical Engineer with Sir Henry Fowler (Midland) as his deputy. There was a subtle change in responsibilities under the new regime in that the C M E was not responsible for locomotive running such duty falling upon the Chief General Superintendent, a position allocated to J. H. Follows (Midland). Therefore two ex-Midland men, Sir Guy Granet and J. H. Follows held prominent positions which allowed them a strong voice in the way the company was run. It soon became evident that the Midland way prevailed and this resulted in the 1923 amalgamation being known as 'Midlandisation'.

All locomotives were assigned a new livery of Midland red and numbering was altered in that L & NWR engines started at 5,000 - L & YR engines at 10,000 - Midland engines retained their existing numbers and Scottish engines commenced at 14,000. Initially, the numbers were painted in large figures on either side of the tender or tank with a cast iron number plate on the smoke box door.

George Hughes

George Hughes had decided to retain Horwich as his headquarters which did not go down too well with the Board. Representatives of various firms along with those visiting him on company business were not pleased with the difficulty involved in travelling to see him. As CME, Hughes had a personal coupé locomotive with the L & YR Works No. 731. When the new numbering system was introduced he insisted that the coupé carry number 10,000.

On the 29th November 1923, George Hughes recommended to the LMSR Board that the company manufacture of steel should be concentrated at Crewe which was adopted and resulted in the closure of the steel foundry at Horwich which then had a capacity to produce 12,000 tons of ingots per annum.

When the LMSR was originally formed the company had four locomotive workshops situated at Horwich, Crewe, Derby and St. Rollox, Glasgow; respectively. With the appointment of Sir Josiah Charles Stamp as President of the Executive from the 1st January 1926, economies were sought in the locomotive and running departments to avoid unnecessary duplication. George Hughes had also submitted detailed, costed plans for the re-organisation and re-equipment of Crewe works which so impressed the Board that they were implemented. The General Strike of 1926 delayed the building work somewhat but the alterations at Crewe were finally completed in 1928.

The knock-on effects at Horwich were that the telegraph, signal and points crossing shops, along with the forge were closed. Operations in the spring smithy were transferred to the general smithy with the vacant shop then being used for the storage of tubes and bars. On the positive side, two of the 30 ton overhead cranes in the erecting shop were replaced by cranes capable of lifting up to 50 tons, during 1925. (a further two 50 tonners were added in 1954). The high level boiler house was also closed about 1927 but this was because electricity had replaced steam and thus rendered the boiler house obsolete.

There is no doubt that George Hughes felt that his efforts were to some extent in vain particularly in view of the dominance which the Midland Railway seemed to hold over affairs after the 1923 groupings. He is reported to have clashed on a number of issues with Sir Henry Fowler, his deputy at Derby. Both Hughes and Fowler had strong connections with Horwich and it is sad that professional differences should have soured those friendships. Nevertheless, both men continued a particular acquaintance with Samuel Drinkwater, the Leading Draughtsman at Horwich Locomotive Works and the three personal letters reproduced provide a unique insight into their relationship.

Samuel Drinkwater was a Leading Draughtsman at Horwich under George Hughes. He was extremely competent and maintained close links with both George Hughes and Henry Fowler. When George Hughes retired he went to live in Cromer, Norfolk, where he had Samuel Drinkwater design his extensive greenhouses. A copy of a personal letter from George Hughes to Samuel Drinkwater is included along with one from Sir Henry Fowler.

Letter from Sir Henry Fowler to Samuel Drinkwater, dated 26 July 1933.

TELEPHONE: SPONDON 61.

SPONDON HALL,
Nr. DERBY.

July 26th 1933.

Dear Sam,

I was very delighted - as you will know - when a note came this morning from Mr Shawcross saying your son had got a Whitworth Scholarship. I take it that this is the first one a really Horwich trained fellow has got. Will you offer him from me my very heartiest congratulations & best wishes for his future. I shall look forward to seeing him at the dinner of the Whitworth Society to which he will be invited.

As you will know I am all the more delighted that this first - long waited for distinction has come to the son of one of my old students.

With kind regards
Yours sincerely
Hy Fowler.

64 Scholes Bank
Horwich
30th July 1933

Dear Sir Henry

My son John Wilson and I thank you for your heartiest congratulations and best wishes for his future, for having got a Whitworth Scholarship.

It is very kind of you to look forward to seeing him at the dinner of the Whitworth Society to which you say he will be invited.

It is also very nice of you to think of old times - you see your tuition has borne fruit in the next generation. I look with pride on the four books you gave me for homework prizes in applied Mechanics and Steam Engines, I have obtained valuable information from them in my vocation.

I am pleased to say my second son Geoffrey has obtained his Higher National Certificate this year before the completion of his apprenticeship.

With kind regards to you and Lady Fowler
Yours sincerely
Sam Drinkwater

Letter of reply from Samuel Drinkwater to Sir Henry Fowler dated 30 July 1933.

Letter from George Hughes to Samuel Drinkwater
dated 19th September 1937.

19:9:37
West Lawn,
Cliff Avenue,
Cromer,
Norfolk.
Tel. 175.

My dear Drinkwater

In this weeks Journal I see a happy smiling face, just you as ever, and a jolly group. I hope the young people will be very happy. The Greenhouse is going as strong as ever. Well built, to a splendid carefully prepared drawing. The boiler has just given out, otherwise not a single leak in the joints of the system. When you see Gass tell him that I hear he is very busy over Super-heater patents & I hope he will get something out of his scheming. I hope you & all of yours are well. Kind regards & best wishes —

Yours faithfully,
Geo. Hughes

Letter from the Horwich R.M.I. Amateur Photographic Society to John McLean, Librarian of the Mechanics' Institute on his retirement.

Horwich R. M. I. Amateur Photographic Society.

Federated with R.P.S. L & C.P.U. I.C.A.

Hon. Secretary
S. Walkden,
2, Hilton Avenue,
Horwich.

President
S. H. Whitelegg Esq.

OCTOBER 10th, 1929.
14 Crown Lane
Horwich

J. MC. LEAN, ESQ:
Dear Sir,

The Committee desire to express their sincere appreciation for the kind help which you have at all times so willingly given, and it is their heartfelt wish that you may be blessed with good health, in which to enjoy a long, happy, and well earned retirement.

Believe me, Dear Sir,

Yours faithfully,

C. H. Smith

Asst. Hon. Sec.

The letter from George Hughes (included) mentions the boiler in the greenhouse at his Cromer home which was designed and fitted by Samuel Drinkwater. George Hughes was a keen horticulturist and is remembered as an approachable unassuming man. He took early retirement from his post as CME in 1925 when he moved to Cromer where he advised on defence work. He finally moved to Stamford, Lincolnshire, where he died on the 27th October 1945 aged 80 years. In his obituary notice which appeared in the Engineer dated 2nd November 1945, reference is made to a treasured photograph of him as an horticulturist which was framed together with a sketch he had made of one of his locomotives emitting a plume of tomatoes from its chimney. The obituary closes with the comment, "Dear George Hughes".

The author, E. S. Cox, started his career as a premium apprentice at Horwich Locomotive Works during 1917, obtaining lodging accommodation in Fox Street. In his book 'Locomotive Panorama' (Volume I) he recounts an amusing anecdote concerning a test to determine which steam whistle among the many in use on the newly amalgamated railways was the best. Apparently the test was scheduled for the 18th December 1923, when several ex- CME's including Sir Henry Fowler and Major H. P. M. Beames assembled on the Red Moss at Horwich to judge the steam whistles which were set up on steam pipes fed by the work's boiler. The sight of those men in the depths of winter on what is described as 'probably the bleakest place in Lancashire' had its humorous side particularly when the steam pressure was too low and condensation prevented the tests being properly carried out. The expressions on the faces of that elite assemblage on their return from the aborted mission apparently spoke volumes. There is little doubt that George Hughes would have appreciated the funny side of this incident. In the event, the Caledonian Railway whistle was chosen but its use was short lived because two senior LMSR personalities, Anderson and Follows, were almost deafened by the whistle one day in Manchester Victoria Station and, after enquiry, ordered its removal because the Board had not sanctioned its use.

Locomotive construction at Horwich following the Groupings.

Horwich Locomotive Works continued to build locomotives already on order at the time of the merger, including 41 Hughes 4-6-0s and ten L & YR designed 'Baltic' tank engines. During 1926 the first 2-6-0 mixed traffic tank engine, known as the Horwich Crab, left the works under LMS number 13,000.

John Robert Billington

John Robert Billington was born at Freckleton, Lancashire, on the 18th April 1873 and received his education at Kirkham Grammar School. Following a period of employment with Thomas Riley, a local private contractor who undertook railway company work, Billington began an apprenticeship at Horwich Locomotive Works in 1889, when John A. F. Aspinall was CME. Billington was an extremely gifted individual who secured a number of academic honours including the coveted Whitworth Exhibition which was awarded to him in 1897. He held a number of posts at Horwich until 1913 when he became Chief Draughtsman on the retirement of Zachariah Tatlow. Among the many projects in which he was involved was the design of the 2-6-0 Horwich Crab which was one of the finest locomotives ever designed. His death occurred on the 22nd March 1925 at the relatively young age of 51.

John Robert Billington with his wife. c.1910.

171

H. E. O'Brien

H. E. O'Brien, who was Works Manager and Electrical Engineer at Horwich, read a paper to the Institute of Electrical Engineers during 1924 entitled, ' The Future of Main Line Electrification on British Railways', in which he strongly recommended electrification of the Euston to Carlisle route. He supported his argument with sound technical data and to some extent was ahead of his time in the proposals he put forward. On hearing of the paper, the LMSR Board interpreted O'Brien's actions as an attempt to interfere in policy matters and he was suitably admonished. This led to O'Brien tendering his resignation and he left Horwich to live in Killiney, near Dublin, where for twenty years he lectured on transport at Trinity College. His death occurred at his home in October, 1967, but before he died he was visited by Harold Pendlebury, who was born in Horwich and worked as a journalist for the Daily Mail. A report of this meeting is contained in the local journal dated Friday 29th September 1967 and it is obvious that O'Brien had not forgotten the people of the Horwich. His words to Mr. Pendlebury on that occasion form the dedication for this book.

Depression in the 1930s

The major financial slump of the 1930s hit British industry extremely hard. The new steelworks at Crewe Locomotive Works was closed down when Sir Josiah Stamp, then Chairman of the LMSR, reached agreement with a number of leading 'iron-masters' that the English steel industry would provide all the steel for the company's needs for ten years at 10% less than the current prices. This agreement resulted in the 400 men employed in the steel foundry at Crewe losing their jobs.

At Horwich, locomotive building was suspended following the completion of a batch of 0-6-0 tanks on the 15th October 1931. Operations were then confined to the repair of locomotives. The closure of Newton Heath Works in April 1932 resulted in Horwich becoming responsible for the repair of electrically powered locomotives from the Liverpool - Southport line. This work was undertaken in the north-west part of the erecting shop which was eventually renamed the car shop.

Post War decline in the use of the Railways

The complex problems arising as a result of the 1923 Groupings demanded so much attention that the railway companies were slow to react to the increasing competition from the roads for both passenger and freight traffic.

During the First World War the use of petrol-driven vehicles had escalated to an unprecedented level and whereas before the war only the electrically driven tramcar posed any threat in relation to passenger traffic, bus companies were being formed and road haulage firms using motor lorries vied for the carriage of goods. The ownership of private motor vehicles was also becoming more common.

Railway companies were authorised by Government to set up bus undertakings but took little advantage of this option. They were, however, severely restricted by legislation in being able to increase fares and rates which proved a disadvantage when competing with the mushrooming road transport. The 1926 General Strike and the depression suffered in 1929 / 1930 compounded troubles on the railway in that there remained a legacy of ill-feeling between the management and the workers.

Increased running costs could not be passed on to the consumer by railway companies which resulted in mounting losses. Road haulage firms and bus companies were allowed this concession which made the competition unfair. A direct result of this situation was that between 1923 and 1947 some 1,240 miles of uneconomic railway track were closed.

In order to redress the balance and ensure fairer competitive trading between road and rail companies, the big four railway concerns sought Government sanction to fix their own fares and rates. The subject was still under debate when the Second World War broke out.

Retirement of George Nuttall Shawcross, Works Manager at Horwich Locomotive Works - 1936.

One of the first two Lancashire and Yorkshire Railway buses originally used to open a service between Crosby and Thornton in 1907 but which eventually operated from Chorley Railway Station.

HORWICH LOCOMOTIVE WORKS DURING THE SECOND WORLD WAR 1939 / 1945

Prior to the Second World War the London Midland and Scottish Railway was the largest of the big four companies formed at the groupings in 1923. The operations of the L.M.S. Railway extended from Goole on the east coast of England to Donegal Bay on the west coast of Ireland; and from Bournemouth on the south coast of England to Thurso on the most northerly tip of Scotland. The company owned 7,500 railway engines and 303,000 separate pieces of rolling stock to service some 19,000 track miles. In addition to the company's workshops, a myriad of secondary operations extended the property ownership to docks, harbours and piers, steamships, hotels, canals, dwelling houses, aeroplanes, etc. The traditional railway passenger and freight business employed 250,000 staff with an extensive range of additional employees servicing the ancillary functions.

The outbreak of the Second World War was seen as a distinct possibility long before war was actually declared. As early as 1937, the railway workshops in the Midlands and North were involved in fitting out ambulance trains to carry both service and civilian casualties. The design of a medium tank and, later, the manufacture of aeroplane parts and repair of aircraft were also undertaken. The threat of aerial bombardment resulted in the camouflaging of the workshops and the mass evacuation of many of the largest cities was planned originally in the autumn of 1938 with final refinements for the exercise being made during July 1939.

On the 1st September 1939 Poland was invaded by German forces and on this date the Government took control of the railways. A Railway Executive Committee had been formed to provide the linkage between the Minister of War Transport and the railways companies, acting as advisor to, and agent of, the Minister, to ensure both the smooth running of the war effort and the continued provision of a civilian rail service. At 11.00 a.m. on 3rd September War was declared between Britain and Germany as from 5.00 p.m. that day. The mass evacuation of children from the cities took place between the 1st and 4th September with 1,200,000 persons being moved in England and Wales. The L.M.S. Railway operated 1,450 special trains over this period and moved approximately half a million children.

The building of new locomotives and carriages was largely suspended with the outbreak of hostilities although Government orders were relatively small until April 1940. This period of inactivity in the workshops led to many skilled and unskilled men leaving to either join the services or take up more remunerative employment elsewhere.

Whereas in the First World War Horwich Locomotive Works was principally involved in the production of fuses and shells and the renovation of cartridge cases; its responsibilities in World War Two were much more diverse. Women were once again employed in numbers to augment the workforce. Some 600 women made up the complement of 2,328 employees at Horwich Locomotive Works. The Forge was vacated and used as the Cartridge Case Reform Plant where much of the female labour was occupied. Throughout the duration of the war Horwich Locomotive Works produced 6,740,000 oerlikon shells and renovated some 18,713,000. A further 4,333,000 - 3.7 and 4.5 shell cases were also renovated. Additionally, 481 tanks were manufactured, comprising 406 (Waltzing) Matilda Mk. II tanks, 45 Centaur tanks and 30 Cruiser tanks. A variety of aircraft parts were also produced.

During 1939 the Railway Mechanics' Institute was used to billet troops. Unfortunately the largely wrought iron bandstand in the recreation ground was dismantled for scrap to assist the war effort.

In recognition of Horwich's contribution to the war effort King George VI and Queen Elizabeth visited the town on 2nd May 1940.

From May until November 1943, a total of 33 American 2-8-0 railway engines received some 30 modifications in the erecting shop at Horwich Locomotive Works. In June 1943 the suspension on locomotive building was lifted and work commenced on a batch of Stanier 2-8-0s and tenders.

Shell manufacture and re-furbishment at Horwich Locomotive Works

The photographs below give some indication of the sterling efforts of local women during the period of hostilities.

Royal Visit to Horwich, Thursday, 2nd May 1940. The King and Queen are pictured on Horwich Railway Station together with Railway Company officials and members of the armed services.

King George VI and Queen Elizabeth on their visit to Horwich on 2nd May 1940. The crowds in Church Street welcome the Royal visitors.

A (Waltzing) Matilda Mk. II. Tank manufactured at Horwich Locomotive Works during wartime.

An American 2-8-0 railway engine which received modification in the erecting shop at Horwich Locomotive Works.

NATIONALISATION

The effects of World War II left the railways of Britain in a deplorable state. Apart from direct losses sustained as a result of enemy action, which included the destruction or damage of 14,000 passenger vehicles and 24,000 freight wagons, the operations were severely affected by aerial bombardment. Some 247 stretches of railway track were rendered inoperable for a week or more. The unprecedented demand for railway services reached a peak in 1944 when 178,000 special trains were run, mainly in connection with the invasion of France. The commitment of the railways to the war effort did not end with the signing of peace because as late as September 1946 an average of 550 special troop trains and 300 freight trains were being operated weekly on behalf of the Government.

At the General Election, held just after the war, a Labour Government was returned to office. One aspect of Labour policy was the public ownership of national undertakings. It was natural therefore that the Nationalisation of the railways was sought and in furtherance of this objective the Transport Act of 1947 was placed before Parliament. The Bill sought authorisation to purchase compulsorily the railways of Britain which it was intended would be managed by a newly created body known as the British Transport Commission. There was much heated debate on the subject, and, sadly, the enormous contribution of the railways in securing victory was denigrated. The purpose of the criticism was in effect a bargaining ploy to secure the railways of Britain at the lowest possible price.

There is little doubt that the railway companies would have had an almost impossible task in their attempts to recover services to pre-war standards. The arrears of maintenance to be completed and the amount of re-equipment necessary, were in themselves a daunting proposition but coupled with an acute shortage of money and an even scarcer supply of materials the prices of which were rising steeply, the cost of recovery seemed prohibitive.

On 6th August 1947 the Transport Act received the Royal Assent. The four major railway companies continued operations until midnight on the 31st December 1947 when, along with the London Passenger Transport Board which had the responsibility for rail in the capital city, they ceased to exist and British Railways came into being.

It was not practicable to operate the railway system as a single entity so the Commission formed seven regions one of which covered the London area. Perhaps the most radical change was the creation of Scotland as a region of its own under the directorship of the Chief Regional Officer for Scotland. All railtrack north of the border once owned by the L.M.S. and the L.N.E.R. respectively was now controlled by the Scottish region.

HORWICH LOCOMOTIVE WORKS FOLLOWING NATIONALISATION

The seven regions comprising the British Railways network were the Scottish, North Eastern, Eastern, Western, London Midland, Southern and the London Region. The LMSR lines in Northern Ireland continued to be administered by the Northern Counties Committee until 1949 when the, then, newly formed Ulster Transport Authority purchased the operation. Horwich Locomotive Works became a workshop for the London Midland Region.

Henry George Ivatt, the son of Henry Alfred Ivatt who had served his apprenticeship with John A. F. Aspinall at Crewe during the 1860's became Chief Mechanical and Electrical Engineer of the London Midland Region on the 1st January 1948. He had previously held the post of CME on the LMSR and amongst his notable achievements was the design of Britain's first diesel-electric locomotive No. 10,000 which left Derby workshops in December 1947.

Orders for new locomotives at Horwich Locomotive Works prior to nationalisation were confirmed by British Railways. These included the manufacture of LMSR Class 5 mixed traffic 4-6-0 locomotives known as Black Fives. This type of engine, originally introduced in 1934, was a veritable workhorse and 842 Black Fives were constructed between 1934 and 1951. Although H. G. Ivatt was in favour of diesel engines he felt that the Black Fives still had an important role to fulfil and authorised their continued construction with some modifications including Caprotti valve gears and Timken roller bearing axle boxes fitted to the coupled wheels. It is significant that at this time all heavy forging needed for new locomotives built at Crewe, Derby and Horwich, were produced solely at Crewe.

The end of the Second World War signalled a period of rationalisation within the newly created British Railways. It was essential that the concern was self-financing which necessitated a complete review of the system to cut out waste and avoid duplicity in the operations of the workshops.

British Railways categorised work done in its various workshops as the building of new engines, heavy repairs to engines, light repairs and repaired boilers. A heavy repair was defined as an occasion when a locomotive had to be reboilered or the boiler taken out for general repair in addition to any two of the following: (a) four or more wheels fitted with new tyres, (b) new cylinders fitted, (c) new axle or axles in engine and tender fitted, (d) re-tubing, (e) either turning-up wheels and re-fitting boxes or motion and brake work stripped and overhauled, (f) boiler repaired whilst still in the frame but with not less than 50 stays renewed. From the criteria it can be seen that to qualify as a heavy repair major work had to be completed. A typical years work at Horwich Locomotive Works taking 1953 as an example was 347 heavy repairs, 314 light repairs, 26 new engines and 164 repaired boilers. A total of 93 repairs were also made to electric stock.

THE MECHANISED FOUNDRY

During the 1950's a mechanised foundry, reputed at the time to be one of the biggest in the country, was installed in what had been the Forge and the Steel Foundry at Horwich Locomotive Works. The mechanised foundry comprised two completely separate mechanised plants, one for producing permanent way chairs and baseplates, and one for the production of brake-blocks and small tonnage of miscellaneous castings. these were known respectively as the Chair Plant and the Brake-Block Plant. The former was opened in September 1950 and the latter in August 1951. By 1952 both plants were working double shift producing an average of 480 moulds per hour in the Chair Plant and 232 moulds per hour in the Brake-Block Plant. Some 488 staff were employed in the two plants.

Exterior view of the Mechanised Foundry. 1961.

Continuous casting in the Mechanised Foundry.

Mould Conveyor - Mechanised Foundry.

CHURCHILL MK. 7 FLAIL TANKS

In the early 1950's Horwich Locomotive Works received a Ministry of Supply contract to provide 72 Churchill Mk. 7 Flail Tanks. The purpose of these machines was to clear the battlefields of mines ahead of advancing infantry. Basically, a Churchill Mk. 7 Tank was stripped of turrets and armament and then rebuilt with raised superstructure. A rotating flail drum was carried in front of the tank on extended booms. The drum was fitted with weighted chains, each chain similar to what can best be described as a ball and chain. As the tank advanced the flails beat the ground in order to neutralise land mines.

Two prototypes of the Flail Tanks were produced at Horwich Locomotive Works during 1952 - 1954. Robinson and Kershaw of Dukinfield converted the original tanks which were then transported to Horwich for completion by the manufacture and installation of the flail mechanism.

A total of 42 Flail Tanks were produced between 1954 and 1956. This number was made up of two prototypes, six interim models and thirty four final design machine vehicles.

The Flail Tanks were never used operationally and were eventually broken up for scrap.

Churchill Mk. 7 Flail Tank under construction in the Chain Smithy at Horwich Locomotive Works.

FROM STEAM TO DIESEL

Experiments involving the use of oil, as an alternative to steam for locomotives, were carried out in Britain and in Russia in the 1870's and 1880's but progress in this field of research was largely ignored because both coal and water were cheap, of good quality and easy to obtain; whereas oil was relatively expensive because it had to be imported. The German engineer, Rudolf Diesel, continued experiments from 1905 and his name is linked with fuel oil. However he did not invent the heavy oil engine but worked tirelessly in achieving its acceptance. The situation changed following the Second World War when coal became increasingly difficult to obtain and therefore more costly. At this time, many other countries, America in particular, were rapidly changing over to diesel traction and viewed steam power as outdated. The main advantages of diesel over steam are that all fuel is of the same quality and there is no variation in consistency of operation, which happened with steam when clinker formed or the coal fired badly. Additionally, no diesel fuel was consumed while the locomotive was stationary.

Orders continued to be received at Horwich Locomotive Works, post-war, for batches of between 10 and 30, L.M.S. 2-6-0 Class 4 with tenders and L.M.S. 4-6-0 Class 5P5F with tenders. Between the 15th November 1945 and the 2nd March 1951 a total of 185 locomotives were ordered; comprising 75 x 2-6-0's and 110 x 4-6-0's.

A further 20 British Railways, Standard 4, 2-6-0 engines with tenders, were ordered on the 1st October 1952; and a batch of 5 L.M.S. 0-4-0 'Dock Saddle Tank' engines were commenced on the 15th September 1953. The 2-6-0 engines ordered on the 1st October 1952 were the last to be manufactured at Horwich Locomotive Works and the final locomotive, No. 76099, left the works on the 27th November 1957.

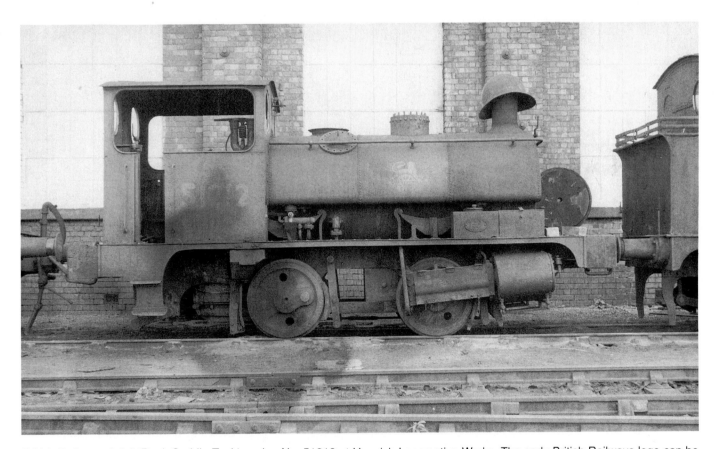

British Railways 0-4-0 'Dock Saddle Tank' engine No. 51212 at Horwich Locomotive Works. The early British Railways logo can be seen in the centre of the saddle tank. The logo was manufactured by Butchers and depicted a lion astride a spoked wheel with the title 'British Railways' across the centre of the wheel. Unfortunately the design came in for much criticism because the lion was so emaciated looking and this led to its nickname of 'the ferret and dartboard'.

On the 20th August 1958, Horwich Locomotive Works began the construction of a series of 350 horse power 0-6-0 diesel shunting locomotives. The rate of build for these locomotives was one every 21 working days. The first to leave the works was numbered D. 3593 and until the 28th December 1962 a total of 169 diesel shunters were manufactured at Horwich. The last one was numbered 4157.

350 H.P. 0-6-0 Shunting Diesel No. 4022 built at Horwich Locomotive Works. The later British Railway logo appears on this engine consisting of a demi-lion rampant holding a wheel between its paws. The words British Railways are on either side of the crest.

Building a new diesel locomotive in the Erecting Shop at Horwich Locomotive Works.

Steam and diesel locomotives stand side by side in the Erecting Shop at Horwich Works.

WORKS TRAINING SCHOOL

The highly specialised repair work carried on at Horwich Locomotive Works required skilled labour, and hence the employment of a considerable number of apprentices. A progressive system of workshop training was needed so that each individual apprentice followed a predetermined schedule according to the trade selected.

In order to fulfil this specialised training a Works Training School was built at Horwich Locomotive Works on an open site near to the main entrance. Accommodation was provided for 72 apprentices to undertake a 12 month training schedule. As a rolling programme 24 boys were inducted at four monthly intervals. When admitted to the Works Training School, each apprentice trainee served a four month probationary period and if successful was allowed to finish the course. On completion of the training programme, trainees were transferred to the workshops as trade apprentices in a situation which depended upon the student's proven ability and aptitude; and the availability of a vacancy in the appropriate workshop.

The foundation stone for the Works Training School was laid on the 25th October 1957 by Sir Landale Train, C.B.E, M.C., of the British Transport Commission. The official opening ceremony was conducted by the Right Honourable Lord Rusholme of the British Transport Commission on the 27th February 1959.

Subsequently the building was extended so that up to one hundred students would be accommodated.

Foundation stone laying ceremony for the
Works Training School, 25th October 1957,
by Sir Landale Train, C.B.E., M.C.

Construction of the Works Training School.

View across the site of the new Training School with Rivington Pike visible in the background. The bridge to the left carries Chorley New Road over the railway track linking Horwich Railway Station with the Horwich Fork Junction.

Official opening ceremony for the new Works Training School conducted by Lord Rusholme of the British Transport Commission on the 27th February 1959.

The administrative block is to the left with the newly completed Works Training School on the right.

Exterior view of the Training School with Rivington Pike on the far right.

Interior view of the Works Training School. Lord Rusholme addresses the students in the Fitting Section at the new school.

The first intake of students at the Works Training School photographed in September 1958.

Works Training School - view of the training workshop,

THE BRITISH RAILWAYS BOARD

One drawback of Nationalisation was that whilst the British Transport Commission had overall financial control of the operations of British Railways, the actual management of railway services was vested in the Railway Executive. The railway system had recovered well immediately following the Second World War and in 1952 an operating surplus of £79 million was achieved but by 1962 the surplus had been replaced by accrued losses amounting to £104 million.

In 1962 the Conservative Government secured the passage of the Transport Act 1962 which effectively abolished the British Transport Commission and replaced it with the British Railways Board. The Board had responsibility for both finance and management. A number of subsidiary Boards were also established, including one solely responsible for London Transport.

Dr. Richard Beeching was the first Chairman of the British Railways Board, who, together with his officers, carried out a review of the railway system to return the operation to solvency. The result was the publication of two reports, 'The reshaping of British Railways' (1963), and 'The Development of the Major Railway Trunk Routes' (1965).

Many of the recommendations contained in the reports were implemented but the return of a Labour Government in 1964 effectively halted further implementation. Dr. Beeching left the Board in 1965 after which he was created a Peer of the Realm. The new Minister of Transport, Barbara Castle, formulated policies for the railways which were embodied in the Transport Act 1968. One aspect of the policies was that a large number of unprofitable lines remained open but they were paid for by the State.

CLOSURE OF HORWICH RAILWAY STATION

In the wake of the 'Beeching Report' on the re-shaping of British Railways a decision was taken to close Horwich Railway Station. At 12 noon on Saturday, 25th September 1965, the last passenger train, pulled by locomotive No. 42626, left the station for Bolton. Goods traffic continued to use the line until final closure on the 25th April 1966.

The site of the railway station lay derelict and neglected until plans were approved for the area to be landscaped and used as linear parkland. The 'Old Station Park' was officially opened by the Town Mayor of Horwich, Councillor S. Dawson, on the 27th September 1980.

Horwich Railway Station Staff. c.1910.

A group of holidaymakers at Horwich Railway Station. c.1955.

BRITISH RAIL ENGINEERING LIMITED

On the 1st January 1970, Horwich Locomotive Works, along with all other railway workshops became part of British Rail Engineering Limited. One positive aspect of the new set-up was that the Works were permitted to tender for outside contract work. In early 1971 Horwich Works successfully tendered for the provision of 'car-lumber platforms' which were, in effect, car transporter frames, 30 feet in length, which were used to transport Volvo cars across the Atlantic. For the return journey the frames were loaded with Canadian timber for the British market - hence the name of the product. An automatic locking device fitted to the frames at Horwich proved useful in reducing labour costs.

Despite receiving orders, the workforce at Horwich, in common with the employees at other workshops throughout the country, felt uncertain about their future prospects in the railway industry. Some relief was felt when the investment of £3 million was announced to upgrade facilities at Horwich Locomotive Works. The mechanised foundry was to be fully automated and a 16 ton mineral wagon re-bodying programme was planned. In addition there was to be increased production of wagon springs and PVC / nylon / polythene sheeting. The introduction of Container building was a further proposal along with extra responsibility for wagon repairs.

Although the proposals did much to dispel the feelings of unease amongst the workers many still felt unsettled. However, in the next five years, the workforce increased from 2,080 to just under 2,500.

Wagon Shop. 1974.

Replica of the locomotive 'Sans Pareil' outside the Erecting Shop at Horich Locomotive Works, 1980.

'Sans Pareil' was originally built by Timothy Hackworth, Foreman of the Stockton and Darlington Railway, to take part in the Rainhill Locomotive Trials staged in the week commencing 5th October 1829. The engine exceeded the $4^{1}/_{2}$ ton weight limit but took part in the trials only to withdraw due to mechanical troubles after completing eight runs. The Trials were won by George Stephenson's 'Rocket'. In order to celebrate the 150th Anniversary of the Rainhill Trials, the Hackworth Locomotive Trust of County Durham, along with six British Rail Engineering Workshops, constructed a replica of 'Sans Pareil'. The patterns for the model and the iron castings required were all manufactured at Horwich Locomotive Works.

CLOSURE OF HORWICH RAILWAY MECHANICS' INSTITUTE.

In the early years of its existence under John A. F. Aspinall the Mechanics' Institute was attended by many men who went on to carve out successful careers in engineering. These included Sir Henry Fowler, Sir Nigel Gresley, A. V. Roe and John Robert Billington.

The Government gradually began to realise that the provision of technical education was as important as learning the three R's and should not be left in the hands of private companies to provide. There began a pursuit of policies to establish sound technical education on a national basis.

During 1919 the Mechanics' Institute became affiliated with the Worker's Education Committee and ten years later, in 1929, a Junior Technical School was opened at the Institute with an intake of 25 boys aged 13+ years. This initiative was the first of its kind in Lancashire and proved extremely successful.

Initially, the funding for the provision of technical education at the Institute was provided by the railway companies but the County Council eventually financed teaching salaries and the cost of educational equipment, whilst the accommodation at the Institute continued to be provided free of charge. This situation existed until 1937 when the London Midland and Scottish Railway Company, who then owned the Mechanics' Institute, relinquished control of educational matters to Horwich Higher Education Committee. The payment of rent and rates for the Institute then became the responsibility of the County Council.

In 1958 the Mechanics' Institute was officially handed over to the British Rail Staff Association. In order to provide social facilities for members the old reading room and library were converted into a concert room and bar.

A new technical school, known as Horwich Technical College, was built on Victoria Road and opened during 1961. The teaching of technical subjects was then transferred from the Mechanics' Institute to the new school. This included the Junior Technical School section. Classroom accommodation at the Institute was retained by the County Council to augment that provided by Horwich County Junior School.

Club premises were constructed for the members of the British Rail Staff Association, at the junction of Chorley New Road and Ramsbottom Road, which opened in October 1969. The only use of the Institute was then the provision of additional classroom facilities which became less and less necessary and finally, in June 1974, the Education Authority abandoned the need.

Several efforts were made by British Railways to sell the building but there were no takers and the Institute remained closed and shuttered for two years during which time it was the target for vandals.

On the 6th October 1976 a fire broke out in the basement of the building which quickly spread. Nearby residents had to be evacuated from their homes as firemen fought to bring the blaze under control and traffic was diverted because of falling debris. In the event, the premises were totally gutted and demolition was the only option.

Bolton Metropolitan Borough Council had in fact purchased the Mechanics' Institute and associated land from British Railways in August 1976 for £45,000, and it was scheduled for demolition in November 1976. The cost of demolition was however doubled because material which could have been salvaged by the demolition company was destroyed.

Following demolition, the site was re-developed by the North British Housing Association who constructed residential housing including sheltered accommodation for the elderly.

The stone from the Mechanics' Institute which commemorates the gift of the Fielden Wing is presently preserved in front of what was the Works Training School. The Works Training School, incidentally, was closed when Horwich Locomotive Works closed in December 1983. Since this time it has been used by the Bolton Training Group as a management training centre for organisations in all areas of business and commerce.

Fire at the Railway Mechanics' Institute, 6th October 1976.

CHANGING FORTUNES

After the closure of Newton Heath Works in April 1932, the north west end of the Erecting Shop at Horwich Locomotive Works was used for the repair of Electric Multiple Unit vehicles (E.M.U's), and was re-named the Car Shop. As the amount of electrification on the railways spread, the involvement of Horwich in repair and maintenance work increased proportionately. In the early 1960's the Car Shop employed 82 men, and E.M.U's were maintained from the electrified systems in Lancashire, Cheshire and elsewhere. A total of 438 E.M.U's were repaired during 1960, comprising 176 from Liverpool and Southport, 129 from the Wirral, 69 from Manchester, South Junction and Altrincham, 52 from Manchester and Bury; and 12 from the Lancaster, Morecambe and Heysham lines. Maintenance of E.M.U's was carried out in accordance with a four year programme and assistance was also rendered in relation to rolling stock.

Car Shop showing the repair of electric multiple unit vehicles. 1961.

The primary function of Horwich Locomotive Works was the production and repair of locomotives and the Erecting Shop remained the largest in the works, employing 618 staff during the 1960's. Albeit the last steam locomotive manufactured left the works on the 27th November 1957, repairs to the fleet of steam engines still in service on British Railways kept the workshops busy. Steam engine repairs were carried out in three stages - stripping, frame section and finishing. Additional sections of the Erecting Shop were dedicated to the repair of locomotive pony trucks, boiler mounting, repair of tenders, coach bogies and tube repairs.

Erecting Shop - general view. 1961.

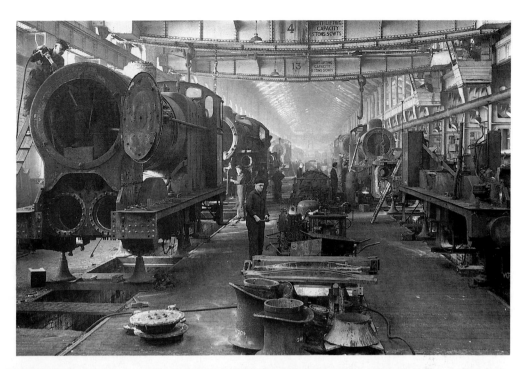

Steam Locomotives under repair in the Erecting Shop. 1961.

With dieselisation, the amount of repair work to steam locomotives began to diminish and the last steam engine to be repaired at Horwich left the works on the 8th May 1964. To some extent the end of steam was inevitable but the effects upon the workforce were ameliorated by the introduction of repair work to diesel engines in late 1957. On the 20th August 1958, work began on the construction of a series of 350 H.P. shunting diesels. A total of 169 shunting diesels were built at Horwich, the last one leaving the works on the 28th December 1962.

Changes in manufacturing techniques and the termination of production lines, generally have an adverse effect on the morale of the workforce. It is a tribute to the locomotive work's staff at Horwich that they responded positively and adapted so well to the changes. The photograph included shows a private moment amongst colleagues which captures the ethos of the British working man.

Horwich Locomotive Work's employees enjoy a Christmas drink in one of the carriages at the works. c. 1950. The following have been identified on the photograph, Mr. Turtington, (front left), George Mercer (holding the bottle), and Jack Marsden (right of centre wearing a cap and holding a glass).

Such radical alteration to working patterns led to reorganisation of the workshops in general. A plan of Horwich Locomotive Works as it appeared in 1961 is included. It gives some idea of the extent to which workshop use altered when compared with the earlier plan of the works.

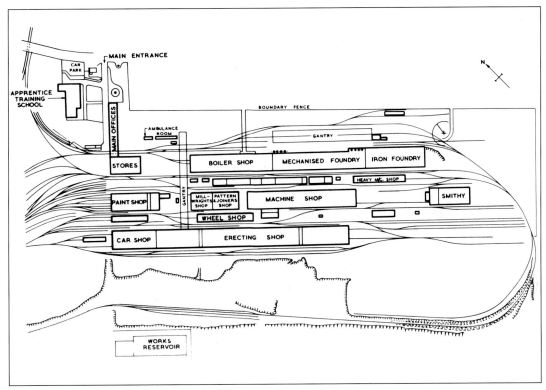

Plan of Horwich Locomotive Works 1961.

Facilities in the Machine Shop were vastly improved following Nationalisation and those at Horwich were amongst the best on British Railways. Operating with a staff of 458, the Machine Shop was responsible for the manufacture of all tools and cutters, including jigs, fixtures, press tools, templates, gauges, cutting tools, etc. Situated at one end of the Machine Shop was a fitting section for brake gear and locomotive details, with a plant for the heat treatment of various details in a separate shop. A repair section for diesel locomotive material was also provided. In an annexe to the main shop a number of large machines were housed for use in the production of locomotive cylinders.

Machine Shop - general view of Capstan Lathe section. 1961.

Machine Shop - Diesel component repair section. 1961.

Although locomotive boilers had ceased to be manufactured at Horwich, repairs to boilers were still carried out. The Boiler Shop comprised three bays and two thirds of one of the bays was eventually in use for boiler repairs. The remaining third of this bay had a welding section for heavy fabrications requiring manipulators, such as locomotive saddles, diesel fuel tanks, radiators and similar assemblies. Plates were prepared in the centre bay of the shop, then marked out and passed to the plating sections. The remaining bay was used for plate flanging and was equipped with a 600 ton hydraulic press and a large producer gas fired furnace.

Boiler Shop - general view of the centre bay. 1961.

Rationalisation of the foundries on the London Midland region of British Railways led to the Iron Foundry at Horwich taking on the production of plate pattern work for other regions in addition to the London Midland. The main products were wagon axle boxes, locomotive fire bars, point and crossing chairs and general castings of a semi-repetitive nature. In total, 102 semi-skilled staff were employed whose approximate weekly output was 150 tons.

Iron Foundry - general view. 1961.

The closure of Gorton Works on the Great Central Railway in 1963 meant that the manufacture of points and crossings re-commenced at Horwich Works.

The final destination for a manufactured / repaired locomotive was the Paint Shop. A great deal of skill and effort was needed to turn out a locomotive with smooth varnished paintwork and correct livery. A total of 64 staff were employed in the Paint Shop during 1960 and, to give an idea of the amount of work undertaken in that year; 130 locomotives and 99 E.M.U's were painted whilst a further 39 E.M.U's received a 'wash and varnish'.

Paint Shop - general view. 1961.

In 1969 the coal burning boilers in the Work's Boiler House were replaced with oil-fired ones. These boilers provided the heating and hot water for the offices and workshops.

Coal wagon outside the Boiler House. c. 1950.

Railway carriages and wagons

Operations at Earlestown Locomotive Works were being run down in the 1960's and this resulted in the responsibility for carriage and wagon repairs being transferred to Horwich. Wagons were built in the Erecting Shop while the Car Shop was retained for repairs to E.M.U's. Sections of the Erecting Shop were laid out with facilities to manufacture and repair all types of wagons including mineral, hopper, freightliner, bogie wagons, and pressure vehicles.

Coupled with the increase in wagon manufacture / repair, was a five year programme, introduced in the Car Shop in 1968, to convert 96 Mk. 1 coaches to overhead electric line maintenance vehicles.

The original plans for Horwich Locomotive Works included a Wagon Works where 1,500 men would have been employed but the proposal was never implemented. It is ironic that towards the end of the life of the works the main responsibility should become the manufacture and repair of railway carriages and wagons. There was a feeling that the works would eventually become Horwich Carriage and Wagon Works but this was not to be the case.

Wagon repair in the Erecting Shop.

Closure of Horwich Locomotive Works

The harbinger of closure came in the spring of 1982 when British Rail Engineering Limited (B.R.E.L) announced a series of redundancies at Horwich Locomotive Works. A spirited campaign by trade unionists was successful in averting closure at this time but many of the workforce feared the worst and some 679 opted for voluntary redundancy between July 1982 and May 1983.

Any hopes of continued employment at the works were dashed when on the 18th February 1983 B.R.E.L announced that the works was to close at the end of the year. Trade unions and local councillors combined their efforts in a campaign to 'Save Horwich'. A great deal of sympathy was felt for the workers and the drastic effects that closure would have on the economy of the township. Sadly all the representations were made to no avail and at 1.00 p.m. on the 23rd December 1983 the last 51 employees left the works at the end of their shift. The Horwich Locomotive Works were finally closed, with the exception of the Mechanised Foundry and the Spring Shop, on the 31st December 1983, with the loss of over 1,000 jobs.

CONCLUSION

Horwich Locomotive Works still exist and a number of the buildings are presently utilised, including the Mechanised Foundry and the Works Training School. Traces of the old railway workshops can still be identified but the rail network around the premises has been removed and become overgrown. It is difficult to imagine that these buildings once constituted such a vibrant centre of railway industrial excellence.

The main entrance driveway showing Horwich Fire Station in the centre with the Works Training School on the left. 1988.

General view of the workshops with the distinctive roof of the Works Training School on the left and Horwich Parish Church Tower - far left. 1988.

Rear view of the Millwrights' Shop, and the Wheel Shop. 1988.

The workshops pictured are (left to right) the Paint Shop, the Sheet Shop and the Erecting Shop. 1988.

Rear view of the Supplies Department and Oil Store. 1988.

The railway lines to the Work's complex have been removed and the land is overgrown. Horwich Leisure Centre stands in the centre of this photograph with the parish church behind. 1988.

A poignant reminder of Horwich Locomotive Works is this derelict railway signal. 1988.

4-6-4 Tank Engine in L.M.S. Livery numbered 11114. Thirty of these engines were ordered from Horwich on the 16th August 1923 but following criticism only ten were produced. The one shown, left the works on the 20th May 1924 and was finally withdrawn on the 18th April 1941.

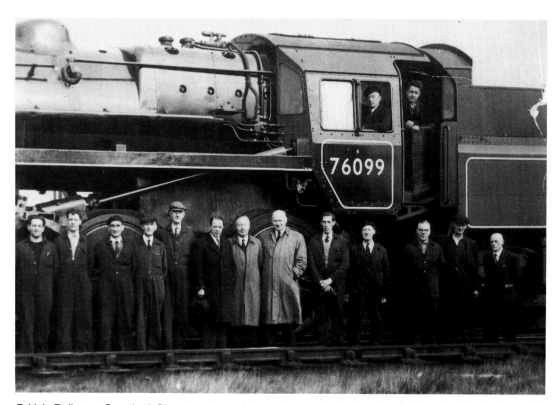

British Railways Standard Class 4 Locomotive No. 76099. This was the last engine built at Horwich Locomotive Works. A.T. Garnett and E.R. Brown, Work's Managers, appear on this photograph taken on departure day, the 27th November 1957.

SELECT BIBLIOGRAPHY

The Lancashire & Yorkshire Railway (3 Volumes) . . . . .John Marshall

The Lancashire & Yorkshire Railway - A concise History . . . . .O. S. Nock

A History of the L.M.S. (3 Volumes) . . . . .O. S. Nock

Crewe Locomotive Works and its men . . . . .Brian Reed

The Aspinall era . . . . .H. A. V. Bulleid

A Regional History of the Railways of Great Britain. Vol. 10. The North West . . . . .Geoffrey O. Holt

The Railways of Britain . . . . Jack Simmons

The L.M.S. at War . . . . .George C. Nash

Britain's Railways at War 1914 - 1918 . . . . .Alan Earnshaw

My Life with Locomotives . . . . 'Rivington'

The Lancashire & Yorkshire Railway . . . . .Eric Mason

Locomotive Panorama. (Volume I) . . . . .E. S. Cox

Check No.
A. Buckley
Kookerup
D. Stuff
23/4/23.
9 a.m.

[L. 112]

Lancashire and Yorkshire Railway.

RULES AND REGULATIONS

TO BE OBSERVED BY

WORKMEN EMPLOYED IN THE LOCOMOTIVE WORKSHOPS.

RULE 1.—TERMS OF ENGAGEMENT.

No Workman will be employed in these Works without a Certificate of Character from his last Employer. He must also produce his National Insurance Health Card, as well as his Unemployment Book, if previously employed in an insured occupation. If these conditions are satisfactorily fulfilled, and the workman's services are required, he will be employed upon his giving a receipt for a copy of these Rules, thus binding himself to observe them, and becoming a member of the Staff's Insurance Society.

RULE 2.—PLACE OF ENTRANCE.

Any Workman entering or leaving the premises by any other way than through the gates at the Time-keeper's Offices will be dismissed.

RULE 3.—CHECKS.

Every man employed has a Check bearing his number. This will be handed to him each time he enters the Works, on passing the Check Office. This Check must be given up each time he leaves the Works.

Anyone neglecting to take up his Check on entering the Works in the morning, or after each meal hour, or to give in his Check every time he leaves the Works, will not be paid for his time. Any man losing his Check will have to pay 3d., the cost of its replacement. The Check Offices will be opened for the issue of Checks at 5-45 a.m., 8-45 a.m., and 1-45 p.m.

RULE 4.—WORKING HOURS.

The week shall consist of 53 hours, commencing at 6-0 a.m. on Friday, and shall be divided as under:—

MONDAY	6 0 a.m. to	8 15 a.m.
TUESDAY		
WEDNESDAY	9 0 a.m. to	1 0 p.m.
THURSDAY		
FRIDAY	2 0 p.m. to	5 30 p.m.
SATURDAY	6 0 a.m. to	10 15 a.m.

No Check will be issued after 6-0 a.m., 9-0 a.m., and 2-0 p.m., except at 6-10 a.m., when the Check Offices will be re-opened for fire minutes to allow those who were too late to take up their Checks, and thereby lose ¼-hour time. The Machinists will leave off 10 minutes before the whistle blows on Saturdays in order to clean the Machines, and will be held responsible for the same being in proper working order. Workmen are forbidden to clean a machine in motion. Any workman committing a breach of this regulation will be severely dealt with.

During meal hours the whole of the Workmen must leave the Works, except when by reason of their employment they have been instructed by their Foremen not to do so.

RULE 5.—PAYMENT OF WAGES.

Wages will be calculated by the hour, and paid on Fridays at 5-30 p.m.

RULE 6.—OVERTIME.

TRADESMEN, MACHINISTS, STRIKERS, PLATE AND MACHINE MOULDERS will be paid for overtime at the rate of time and a quarter for the first two hours, time and a half for the next two hours, and double time afterwards; also double time for Sundays, Christmas Day, and Good Friday. LABOURERS AND GENERAL WORKERS will be paid for overtime at the rate of time and a quarter for first two hours and time and a half afterwards, excepting on Sundays, Christmas Day, and Good Friday, when double time will be paid.

No extra allowance for overtime will be paid until a full day's work has been made.

RULE 7.—APPORTIONMENT OF TIME.

It is the duty of the Time-taker to apportion the time made by the Workmen, who are therefore required to give him correct and sufficient information to enable him to do so.

RULE 8.—ABSENCE FROM WORK.

Any Workman absenting himself from the Works more than one quarter of a day (whether from illness or otherwise) must notify the same to his Foreman, stating the cause of his absence.

Any Workman absent from his employment through lead poisoning must at once notify the same to his Foreman, so that his case can be reported to the Factory Inspector. Any man absenting himself for two days without leave will be considered as having left his employment.

RULE 9.—ACCIDENTS.

ALL accidents, whether they cause personal injury or not, must be reported promptly to their foreman by the workman or workmen concerned.

RULE 10.—FIRE BRIGADE.

Members of the Fire Brigade are required to be prepared and willing to attend instantly, whether for practice or otherwise, whenever called out for that purpose, and it is specially requested that the other Workmen do not discontinue their work, or in any way interfere on such occasions.

RULE 11.—TOOLS.

Every Workman must be provided with such tools as are usual in his trade, and the chest will be examined by the Foreman when the Workman leaves the service.

RULE 12.—INSURANCE OF TOOLS.

Workmen must take steps to insure their own tools. The Company will not be responsible for any tools which may be burnt in case of fire.

RULE 13.—PERSONAL SHOP TOOLS.

Every man will be required to see that each of his shop tools bears the initials of the Company and his own private mark. Every man borrowing tools from another must be careful to return them immediately they are done with. When any Workman requires a new tool he must apply to his Foreman for it, who, if it be necessary, will either supply it or give instructions for it to be made. All new tools must be delivered to the men requiring them by their Foreman, who will receive those they are intended to replace, and no tools must be made or obtained without such authority.

RULE 14.—GENERAL SHOP TOOLS.

Any man using taps, dies, rimers, gauges, or templates must see that, when done with, they are immediately returned, in the same condition as when received, to the person appointed to take charge of them. His not calling the attention of that person to any defects or damage at the time he